Hello Sailor

Michael Hutchinson abandoned an academic career in 2000 to become a full-time cyclist, subsequently winning over thirty national titles. His attempt on cycling's world hour record was the subject of his first book, *The Hour*. He is now a writer and journalist and lives in Cambridge.

Praise for *The Hour*

'Hutchinson proves as good a writer as he is rider (praise indeed) – congenial, funny and insightful . . . A very fine way indeed to spend an hour, any hour.' Matt Seaton, *Guardian*

'[A] warm, gently wise book . . . his prose has gravitas and genuine heroism.' Angus Batey, *The Times*

'Very funny . . . It has the rare quality in any sports-writing of propelling the reader into the intensity of the sporting moment itself.' David Horspool, *Times Literary Supplement*

Hello
Sailor

A Year Spent Adrift and All At Sea

Michael Hutchinson

YELLOW JERSEY PRESS
LONDON

Published by Yellow Jersey Press 2009

2 4 6 8 10 9 7 5 3 1

First published in Great Britain in 2009 by
Yellow Jersey Press
Random House, 20 Vauxhall Bridge Road,
London SW1V 2SA

www.randomhouse.co.uk

Addresses for companies within The Random House Group Limited can
be found at: www.randomhouse.co.uk/offices.htm

The Random House Group Limited Reg. No. 954009

A CIP catalogue record for this book is available from the British Library

ISBN 9780224078801

The Random House Group Limited supports The Forest Stewardship
Council (FSC), the leading international forest certification organisation.
All our titles that are printed on Greenpeace approved FSC certified paper
carry the FSC logo. Our paper procurement policy can be found at
www.rbooks.co.uk/environment

Typeset by SX Composing DTP, Rayleigh, Essex
Printed and bound in Great Britain by
Clays Ltd, St Ives Plc

To the memory of
Tony Dalton

Chapter One
Australia 2

SEEN FROM SPACE THE EARTH IS BLUE. GREAT OCEANS, brushed with accents of swirling cloud, effortlessly outshine the undistinguished-looking lumps of green–brown land. You'd have to be mad to want to live on the green–brown bits. The oceans are clearly places of excitement and romance.

But the closer you get to earth, the more confused the picture becomes. By the time you reach somewhere as earthy as, say, Carrickfergus Sailing Club, situated on a heap of rubble beside a coal merchant's yard on the shores of Belfast Lough, the blue bits have turned an angry grey and the green–brown bit looks like the smart option.

The waters of Belfast Lough are usually this shade of grey. They can do rough grey, and calm grey. But the shade stays the same, and even when it's calm it still somehow manages to look a little menacing. It's a shade that sucks the colour from the surrounding land. You can look across from the club towards Bangor and the grey County Down shore. You can look south-west, to a grey Belfast. And you can look east, to the mouth of the lough, where the grey sea meets the grey sky.

I wasted a youth here. I should have been drinking sweet cider at clandestine parties until I vomited through my ears. Or driving in a souped-up Ford Fiesta at high speed through town centres, looking for all the underage sex with which Northern Ireland was supposedly awash. I should have been storing all the memories away carefully so that when I was old and responsible I would have something interesting to show on the little cinema in my head. Some lucky bastard will have the drunken night when he got his hand down Jessica Jameson's blouse to examine at his middle-aged leisure. All I'll have is the day I got port confused with starboard and crashed my dinghy into a moored boat.

As a child and adolescent, sailing was my heavy metal and my football. I was the kind of obsessive it is only possible to be when you're young. It was always sailing – I didn't pass through any other phases or enthusiasms, only to drop them after a few months. Not unless you're prepared (as I was) to count worrying about sails as a different thing entirely from worrying about masts. There was so much stuff that I accidentally committed to memory. I still keep it in the special bit of my brain where my school wanted me to keep the complete works of William Wordsworth.

For Christmas when I was eleven I got a coffee-table book about the America's Cup. It was not the kind of book you were really supposed to read. It certainly wasn't the kind of book you were supposed to take to bed with you every night for six months. Eventually it fell apart, and I had to keep it in a box. A year or two ago I came across one of its pictures in a magazine advert. The original caption came back like a reflex. I realised that I could begin at the beginning of the book's text and recite it until I, and everyone else in the car, got bored.

And I remember when I turned my back on it all. That I even remember it is remarkable, since it was barely a conscious decision. I was eighteen, and I'd recently arrived at a college in the north-east of England. There was a party in my room – it was not something I'd planned, but the room was on a major thoroughfare and, as I was to discover, it had a tendency to gather up passers-by all on its own. By about nine o'clock most evenings it was full of people whether I liked it or not.

Someone stuck their head around the door, and said there was a call for me on the payphone down the hall – a payphone in a tiny cupboard into which all thirty-five partygoers would rather quaintly try to cram themselves a little later in the evening. The call was from my father, who wanted to give me the phone number of a friend of a friend who raced a boat from a club in Yorkshire, which was manageably nearby.

I tore a bit of paper off a student election poster, and wrote down the number.

'They're racing an autumn series,' said my father, 'so give him a ring as soon as you can.'

I'd been trying – unsuccessfully – to sort out some sailing from the moment I'd arrived in England, and I was delighted to finally have a solid starting point. But somewhere in the dozen steps back to the party, it seemed to lose its importance. Suddenly, the whole idea seemed like more hassle than it was worth. Even if I could have arranged something for the following weekend, well, it

3

was bound to clash with some unmissable excuse to drink to excess and attempt to charm women with my Ian Paisley impersonation. This hadn't yielded the desired result so far, but then again, the term was only a couple of weeks old, and it was a very good impersonation. (Which may, with the benefit of hindsight, have been the problem.)

And the weekend after would be the same – I'd have to abandon the cosy warmth of my new home and all my new friends and get a train to meet a group of strangers, all to spend an hour or two getting doused with North Sea water. I didn't make the decision on my way back from the phone; I only realised that it had already been made. Something in my head had changed, and I'd never even noticed.

I shoved the scrap of paper into a jeans pocket. I knew I'd never see it again. I went back to the party.

I can put a date to the first sailing race I ever won. I kept a diary from the age of eleven, and the entry is easy to find because it's written in the red ink I kept for special occasions, and the margin of the page is decorated with stars:

> I WON! I WON!!! It was great, won by miles, in about a force four wind. Had a Coke and some chips in the club to celebrate. I'm so pleased, it's taken ages to finally win a race. Hopefully I'll win lots more now. Can't wait till the next race.

This was a uncharacteristic outpouring of emotion. I kept a diary that rarely missed a day, but which was very abrupt. A typical effort would be: 'Went to school. It was OK.' Sailing was just about the only thing that got my pen moving.

I could have written a lot more about my win than I did. Perhaps the most reprehensible omission is that it wasn't 'my' win, but 'our' win. My dinghy might have been only 11 feet long, but it took a crew of two. Along with yours truly on helm, mainsheet and being in charge, may I present Stephen Dobbs, on jib trim, spinnaker trim, sarcastic backchat and also, um, being in charge.

If you pluck the wire forestay of a dinghy, the tension produces a note of surprisingly high pitch. That's as nothing compared to the tension between the short, blond, spherical Mr Dobbs and myself. On the night of our (*my!*) first win we managed to put it all aside. This was because for the first time in our relationship, Dobbs had been impressed with my sailing.

About halfway through the race, a bigger, much faster boat – maybe a 30-footer – had overtaken us. From my extensive reading on sailing topics, I knew that if you could get onto one of the quarter-waves in a bigger boat's wake, you could surf along quite happily at something like twice the speed you'd do on your own. Luckily, the bigger boat was heading directly for the next buoy – or 'mark' – we had to round. As it came by, I swerved the dinghy across the wake and onto the quarter-wave.

It was like hopping onto a travelator. We hadn't been doing awfully well in the race until this moment – now we slid past the rest of the fleet (maybe fifteen boats) and off into the lead. None of them worked out what we were up to in time to join us.

It wasn't entirely easy – I had to sail very close to the

bigger boat to stay on the wave, and it took some concentration not to crash straight into them, which would have resulted in disqualification and, almost certainly, a ferocious bollocking from the skipper of the other boat. Behind us, the rest of the fleet shrank into the distance. Dobbs grinned broadly.

We won the race by something like fifteen minutes. Not only did we hitch a ride, the jump that gave us on the rest meant that we had wind all the way to the finish. While we romped home, back down the course our competitors were sitting becalmed, trying to find any breath of air they could. By the time they drifted home we were ashore, with the boat washed and tidied up, and the sails folded. I can't remember exactly, but I suspect we may have been insufferable.

That race was a rare highlight. What might surprise you about trawling through the diary's summer season is just how seldom I managed to win. Sailing is a little like golf – there is a substantial element of luck involved since your motive power – the wind – is not predictable. It can die on one side of the course, but not the other. In light conditions it can come in comical bands and patches that mean you sit under limp sails watching everyone else sailing past just a few metres away.

Even the most talented sailors don't win every race – but they do better on average. That's why most racing comes in the form of a series, which flattens out the luck. Occasionally, a sailor like Ben Ainslie comes along who *can* win race after race, who somehow always manages to pick the right route through shifting winds, who can see what's going to happen next. It's almost impossible to explain to non-sailors just how good he is.

Just as fluctuating winds can sometimes push a star sailor backwards, they can sometimes pull a no-hoper forwards. There were usually only fifteen or so boats racing at Carrickfergus. Even by dumb luck I should have had a couple of victories a season. To the casual observer it must have looked like I was trying not to win. Except that I was trying to win – I've never tried so hard at anything in my life. I consumed books of tactical advice. I got up early to watch Open University programmes on weather. I boned up on the Coriolis effect, and all the good that ever did me was to earn me a detention for arguing with a geography teacher who thought that it had something to do with which way water flowed down a plughole.

I knew all about laminar water flow, turbulent water flow, and how water viscosity changes with temperature. I knew that strange sea conditions off Acapulco mean that the topmost layer of the sea could slide around independently of the water below, so that the top few feet were almost always being blown downwind. This would have been an immensely useful thing to know if there was ever the slightest chance I'd be sailing in Acapulco. As it was, I didn't even know where Acapulco was. I thought it was near Edinburgh, an opinion that when voiced gave my geography teacher one of the happiest moments of his career.

A sailing obsession and a voracious reading appetite was not a good combination. By the time I was twelve, I had raced through all the moderately normal books available, and moved on to undergraduate texts on the finer points of yacht design. Naturally, I started designing. I don't mean drawing boats; I mean T-squares, orthographic projections, calculating displacements, and worrying far into the night about fineness ratios and rudder-tip vortices. Without being unduly immodest, I think I can say that my knowledge of fluid dynamics was unsurpassed by any child of my acquaintance. In one of the small tragedies of which life is stitched together, none of this stuff was ever the slightest use at school.

At school, of course, I stood out from the crowd. I was the one yammering on about sailing all the time. Too much Arthur Ransome meant that sometimes, when I wasn't concentrating, I said things like, 'Oh, let's not be beastly, he's jolly well doing his best.'

Stephen Dobbs actually attended the same school, but most of the time we pretended not to know each other. I think he was worried that a documented friendship with me would be detrimental to his cool. (It's worth mentioning that the most modish thing Dobbs did was play principal trombone in the school orchestra.)

In my daydreams at the back of class, I was a good sailor. Really good. Most of our classes were seated alphabetically, and I was blessed with a tall girl called Emma Hudson who sat in front of me. Wriggling from side to side to keep her between me and the teacher bestowed almost total invisibility, leaving me to drift off behind glassy eyes that saw nothing but a great racing-yacht, foaming through a bright blue sea under a Mediterranean sky. It always had a cloud of sail, and a crew smartly dressed in matching shorts and T-shirts.

The skipper, standing behind a wheel so thrillingly enormous he had to look through the spokes to see where he was going, was always me. I issued crisp orders that were responded to respectfully by the elite crew.

Weaving the winds and the waves and the tides into forward motion, functioning at an almost instinctive level. I would one day be the best there was. It would make me rich. It would introduce me to princes and presidents. It was going to be my life.

I had it planned. I reckoned it would take me until my mid-twenties to get there. I needed to win a national championship in an important dinghy class – that might get me sponsorship to go to some international events, which, naturally, I would shortly thereafter also win. Then I'd go to the 1992 Olympics, and win.

After that I'd make the move out of dinghy racing, where all the top sailors learned their racing trade, to bigger, more glamorous boats, like the one in the fantasy. Within a few years, say by 1995, I'd be at the top of the sport, with multi-millionaire yacht owners queuing up to buy my services as a skipper.

This plan was quite serious. Calculated with all the care that a career deserved, it was miles from the idle fantasising of my friends about playing lead guitar with Iron Maiden. Or at least, that's how it seemed to me. Of course, it was exactly the same, just taken to the next level. I'd gone beyond playing the guitar and was devoting hours to working out the tour dates.

I still had the daydreams long into my secondary-school career, and far past the point where everyone else had devised a halfway normal career plan, and turned their attention to where they might lay their hands on a few tins of Tennent's lager and a girlfriend willing to cushion their disappointment.

Being friends with other sailors would have spoiled this. The rapid decompression involved in walking out of a French class spent sailing off the coast of St Tropez, running straight into Dobbs, and not being able to ignore him would have given me some sort of fantasy version of the bends.

The 1980s were a great time to be a sailing-obsessed kid. For a few years that coincided with my growing up, it was a mainstream sport. Bearing in mind that there were only four television channels, there was a surprising amount of sailing available – from racing coverage, to the slightly duff soap opera *Howards' Way*, to the long forgotten reality show *Cudmore's Call*. This featured Harold Cudmore, a Corkman with a ferocious reputation for aggressive sailing, and an unshakable fixture at number one on my list of personal heroes. In the show he taught a group of celebrities to sail, the idea being that they would then race their boat against Cudmore and his crew. They lost.

No one else can even remember *Cudmore's Call*. I would assume that I'd imagined the whole thing – after all, it was a programme that featured both Harold Cudmore and Annabel Croft, and I was a sailing-obsessed teenage boy. But it also had Eamonn Holmes, and that would have been a rather disturbing bit of casting if it was all down to my subconscious.

All this media interest sprang from the America's Cup, the most prestigious sailing event there is, or ever was. It's always had the most expensive, high-tech yachts, the richest owners, and the best sailors. It's so rarefied that to the outsider it hardly seems connected to the rest of sailing, like Formula 1 compared to all other motor racing.

When the 1983 Cup rolled around, the Americans had

been successfully seeing off all comers for the preceding 132 years – the world of sport's longest winning streak. The first sign that things were going to be different in 1983 was when the Australians turned up with a boat whose apparently unusual keel was always kept hidden. When the boat, *Australia 2*, turned out to be very, very fast, rumours about what exactly they were hiding whirled into a storm of speculation.

The media were quick to pick up on the story. The paparazzi were pulled off the Shakin' Stevens detail, and dispatched to the Cup regatta in Newport, Rhode Island. Surprised hydrodynamics experts were suddenly thrust into the limelight to try to explain what might be going on down there. The keel became, if we exclude the length of pipe found beside Lord Lucan's nanny, the twentieth century's most famous bit of lead.[1]

Suddenly it wasn't just me; everyone was talking about sailing. I was much in demand as an expert on the keel, the America's Cup, yacht-racing in general. And not just from my friends, but from my friends' parents as well, which made me feel even more important. I just loved it. This was the world the way I wanted it to be. I drew little sketches for them, and explained about keel-tip vortices and righting moments.

All of a sudden, people who'd never cared a toss about sailing cared about it passionately. Most passionately of all, they hated the New York Yacht Club, a bastion of WASP privilege of which almost none of them had previously

---

[1] *Australia 2*'s designer was the erratic genius Ben Lexcen, a man with no formal training in design, and who once watched the launch of a yacht he'd designed from the top of a nearby hill with binoculars because he was so scared it was going to sink.

heard, which tried every trick in the book to get *Australia 2* thrown out of the competition. It was the plucky Aussies with the wacky boat versus the duplicitous might of the US. In Newport, Australian supporters took to flying banners showing a kangaroo doing something unspeakable to an eagle. If you weren't American, you were Australian.

The Aussies won, of course. The script couldn't have had it any other way. The celebrations were extraordinary. Australia's teetotal but nonetheless champagne-soaked Prime Minister appeared on television to prohibit employers from firing anyone for failing to show up for work the following morning.

It was the first sporting event I ever cared about. An American victory would have been one of the most traumatic things that my sheltered life had inflicted on me. I mean that. As it was, I celebrated, and the rest of the world celebrated with me. It made me happy for months.

I was always a sailor, but this is what made me an ambitious sailor. Suddenly, my heroes weren't confined to black-and-white photos in the pages of the sailing press, they were proper stars. They had their own TV shows. One day, obviously, so would I.

It was a lot to walk away from, and so casually. It wasn't just my past: it was supposed to be my future. It wasn't so much what I did as who I was.

I think it was like the end of any other love affair: there simply came a moment when however much I'd already committed, it was no longer worth trying to hold it all together. It was just going to cost me too much. There were suddenly so many other things I wanted to do, things that I'd have to give up, all for more of the same. I'd stopped wanting it enough. For someone with my monomaniac tendencies it was an uncharacteristic blink of clarity. It was time to focus on more achievable ambitions.

The irony is that I ended up as a full-time sportsman anyway. After a brief, not awfully brilliant career as an academic, I drifted into cycle racing, turned out to be rather better at it than I'd expected, and took up an offer to do it for money. Well, it seemed like a more alluring means of making a living than trying to explain the role of the Lord Chancellor in the British Constitution to first-year law students. It was one of the very few recorded instances of anyone becoming a professional athlete by accident.[2]

Unlike sailing, bike racing was something I could do, and do well, without having to agonise over it. It just came easily. I had the natural ability that I so painfully lacked when it came to sailing. Within a few months of getting my first racing bike, I was competing in a national championship. It was only when I found out what it felt like to be good at a sport that I realised just how far short of stardom I was always going to have been as a sailor.

What I lacked as a bike rider was, unfortunately, exactly what I had had too much of as a sailor – ambition, drive, a grand plan. I had ability, and I had a fair bit of success, but in the end my cycling career was probably not as successful as it could have been, because most of the time I just bumbled through it, grateful to be paid for something I'd have been doing anyway. In other

---

[2] A story told in more detail in *The Hour*.

words, I had both talent and ambition. Just not for the same sport.

There have been days when I wondered if I was the victim of some sort of cosmic joke. Just whose dream was I living out? Who got mine? Was there really someone, somewhere, who spent their adolescent years fantasising about bike riding, about shiny top-of-the-range racing machines, and about crossing the finishing line with his arms in the air, but who ended up as a professional racing sailor? I once found a tantalising picture in an old book of the bowman on a Canadian America's Cup boat in 1983 wearing a cycling cap. Maybe it was him? I don't suppose I'll ever know.

I didn't go back to sailing. For many years I didn't set foot on any floating object more primal than a cross-channel ferry. But I still thought about it. In my head I could summon up all the sounds, the sights, the smells, the feeling of salt-spray drying and cracking on my face and in my hair. It was something to think about during long training rides on the bike; it helped to pass the time.

I planned to wind down the cycling career in 2006. I was going to do the Commonwealth Games in Melbourne that March, and that would be my last serious event. I didn't plan to quit cycling entirely – I wanted to downgrade it to a hobby rather than a job. It was time to move on.

As you might expect, this decision prompted a certain amount of introspection. I wandered around my mental attic, looking in old suitcases for memories to enjoy, or lost opportunities to grieve over. I thought about what I'd given up for cycling – nights out . . . chips . . . holidays . . . It didn't amount to much. I don't really like nights out, chips or holidays anyway.

When it came to raking through the past, it was to sailing, not cycling, that I kept returning. Sometimes I thought about one or other of my handful of victories. At least as often I niggled at some old failure or humiliation. There seemed to be more of them, and I could remember them more vividly.

I'd given up more for sailing than I ever had for cycling, and for almost no reward at all. People feel sorry for Tiger Woods, for a childhood lost to golf. I put the same work into sailing. Woods emerged from the trauma able to play golf so good that people who play unbelievable golf can't believe it. What did I have? The ability to tie a bowline with one hand. That hadn't proved an indispensable skill in the last fifteen years.

I was cross with my teenage self for his lack of perspective. Then, after a while, I started feeling sorry for him. All that time and effort, and I'd let him down. I'd walked away from everything he'd worked for, abandoning him as a bad job. Despite knowing that logically I'd done the right thing, I felt rather bad about it.

That's where the idea started to form. I had all this sailing-related guilt, the feeling of a job unfinished. And I had a year ahead of me that was empty from the end of March onwards, after I got back from Australia. In other words, about the beginning of the sailing season . . .

It was as subliminal as deciding to give up in the first place. I would go back. I would take my year out, and go back to the sport I loved first. I might fall for it all over again; I might hate it. But it seemed important to find out.

When I went to my parents' that Christmas, I dug some of my old scrapbooks out of the loft, and some particularly prized magazines. On grey, windy Co. Down afternoons in the endless week between Christmas and New Year, I looked at twenty-year-old pictures of famous racing-yachts, foaming along on a blue Mediterranean sea below a blue Mediterranean sky. Behind the wheel and manning the winches were my old heroes. Most of them were younger than me now. They wore matching crew T-shirts, shades, the whole works.

That was where I wanted to be: one of the pros. I wanted it as much at that moment as I had years before. I began to see my year as a last chance. Could I get there? Was there still time to be a pro? It seemed a bit far-fetched to imagine I'd manage in just a few months something that had eluded me before.

On the other hand, the one and only thing my sailing had never lacked was ambition.

Chapter Two

33208

THE WHOLE SAILING OBSESSION WAS MY PARENTS' fault in the first place. In that I was typical, because sailing passes down through families. A lot of the dinghy racers at Carrickfergus had parents racing bigger boats at the club – Stephen Dobbs was something of an exception to the rule. Most of the time he was sailing, his parents thought he was having trombone lessons.

My father had started sailing sometime in the 1960s, and had done a mixture of racing and cruising with friends. He'd given it up to start a business, only to take it up again a decade later, not long after I had started putting my new skills of walking and talking to use by following him around asking a never-ending string of questions of the 'why is the sky blue?' variety. I did this because I adored my father, but in retrospect I can understand why he might suddenly have appreciated the peace of the open sea.

Dad grew a Captain Birdseye-style beard, and bought a little 22-foot fibreglass boat that even to my admiring eyes looked like a bath with a lid and a mast. It was mostly white, with a sort of yellow stain around the waterline that could not be removed with any amount of fibreglass polish. Not by a three-year-old anyway, however forceful the parental exhortation.

The only thing I really remember about this boat was spending ten hours waiting for the tide to come back in after Dad and a friend (and me, though at the age of three my role was limited) ran it aground on some mudflats. Dad's friend swore to the perfection of his navigation, and insisted that an earthquake had moved the seabed. I have, over the intervening years, come to doubt this explanation.

The bathtub spent most of its time on Lough Neagh – the biggest lake in the British Isles, and just about the least prepossessing. Essentially it's a car-park puddle twenty miles by nine and for the most part only about thirty feet deep, complete with its own breed of flying, biting insect. Its sole merit was that it was ten minutes down the road from home. (Every so often the local authorities have a go at turning it into a tourist attraction, apparently blind to the fact that it has all the natural charm of a provincial shopping centre.)

It was to the lough's shore that Mum used to take me on a Sunday afternoon when Dad was racing, to confidently point out the boat and claim he was winning. She was almost always wrong, but I never liked to correct her. We would sit and eat ice-cream from a little café, and wait to wave to Dad and the couple of friends who crewed for him as they came ashore. Dad set a family pattern by winning far fewer races than the laws of probability suggested.

He did take me on the boat once or twice. But I was only ever going to be in the way, and I had to spend the races down below in the little cabin, trying to keep warm, and hold my paper steady enough to draw pictures of Daddy at the Helm, as seen through the hatch. The beard was getting quite bushy by now. It was easy to draw.

After a year or two he decided he needed a bigger boat. That meant moving his sailing to the sea at Carrickfergus, where there was deeper water and more serious racing. He managed to recruit some better sailors to his crew, and the dates on the handful of trophies that reside in a cardboard box in my parents' loft suggest this produced an upturn in his fortunes.

This was the pattern as I grew up. Dad upgraded his boat a few times over the years, but stayed Carrick based. He would disappear for periods of time, varying from a day to a week, to go racing. I'd stay at home with Mum, furious that I'd been left behind.

I hated being a child. I don't mean I had an unhappy childhood, I didn't. It wasn't exactly travelling the world capturing wild animals, but it was all right. I just mean I hated being a child. It was the start of a life-long conviction that everyone else is having more fun than me. Adults always seemed to be doing the things I wanted to do but wasn't allowed to: mowing the lawn, driving cars, going sailing. It seemed telling that none of the adults wanted to do any of the things that they felt it was so important that I do: going to school, learning how to do long division, being quiet.

I think the sailing fixation took hold because it was an adult activity that I could sort-of do. I could go sailing sometimes. I could understand how it worked. I had my own life jacket – so I was already a sailor of some sort, even if the life jacket did have a very frustrating handle on the back by which I could be picked up and carried about.

I think the genesis of my obsession was that simple. But it rapidly became self-perpetuating – a sailor was what I was, and sailing was what I did. The story my school demanded each Monday morning about 'What I did at the Weekend' was always the same – I went to see the sailing boats. Everyone else went to visit their grand-parents, but at least they were smart enough to keep the teacher interested by making something up. I laboured under the conviction that everyone else found sailing as fascinating as me.

It never once occurred to me that I would be anything short of brilliant when I finally got my first command.

My first command, the boat that I was to sail for several seasons at Carrickfergus with Dobbs, was a surprise Christmas present when I was twelve. And it really was a surprise. It remains the only time in my life I've been speechless.

She was a Mirror dinghy, sail number 33208, with a black hull. She – and to me most boats are 'it's – was the most wonderful thing I'd ever seen, even out of her element, parked in my parents' garage in the midst of a Northern Irish winter with snow on the ground outside. I used to dress warmly, and stand in the garage for hours just looking at her under the flattering glow of a 40-watt bulb. It was love. I spent most of the Christmas holidays there. Eventually Mum brought me out a chair.

The Mirror dinghy was so named because its origins

were in a 1963 *Daily Mirror* campaign to bring sailing to the masses. The idea was to produce a cheap dinghy that could be built at home – in essence a flat-pack boat. For the kind of DIY boat builder who can't get a shelf to stay on a wall, the pointy bit you might expect to find at the front of the boat would be fraught with difficulty, so Mirrors have a flat bow. This is technically called a pram bow, and made my love look a little bit more like a big shoebox than I would have wished. In this manly context, I wasn't completely sure I liked the word 'pram' either.

Mirrors are small, uncomfortable, slow and not awfully pretty. They were sailing for the masses only as long as the masses were under about 5 foot 4 and didn't mind travelling at walking pace while the top of the gunwale wore a groove in their buttocks. Ten years old, like *33208*, they didn't cost much more than a half-decent bicycle. She was, I hardly need to add, beyond both price and beauty.

I was like a little girl with a pony. As soon as the snow melted and it stopped raining, somewhere around early May, I brought her into the garden on a calm day and rigged her. With her sails up she was so lovely that I cried.

I sailed her with a friend on Lough Neagh for a few weeks that summer. Not racing – just going out for a sail, practising the basics, tacks and gybes, trimming the sails. I can remember warm spring days, with the northern daylight lasting far into the evening, giving the calm lake a silvery sheen. Occasionally we'd set ourselves a course round some buoys, to give the thing a bit more purpose. But more often we just ambled, letting *33208* sail herself while we swapped what we imagined to be dirty jokes.

We'd sail until the sunset started to glow orange, then

cycle home flat-out to make it back before it was completely dark, arriving with dead midges speckled over our faces and items of hastily packed sailing kit spilling out of our rucksacks. Looking back at it now, it seems like a bit of childhood that had leaked out of another era, from a golden inter-war summer of macaroons and cream teas.

Our own private 1930s lasted for just a few weeks. Alistair went on a family holiday for July and August, and I was left crewless. Since Dad was travelling back and forth to Carrickfergus to sail his boat, it made sense to take *33208* there instead. I could start my sailing career in earnest. Oh, the optimism. Someone introduced me to Stephen Dobbs, and the ghastly rot that characterised my dinghy-racing career set in.

There were ways in which sailing on the sea at Belfast Lough wasn't quite like the thing everyone else seemed to be doing in the magazines and books. A diary entry from that August:

> Second again! Paul and Mike, and Samantha and Connor had spinnaker trouble with the flies, and then got caught up in the jellyfish on the next beat. Only the Smiths and ourselves avoided them all. Really pleased.

In an evening race in light winds, little black flies would settle in their thousands on a light-coloured sail. Eventually their weight would cause the sail to collapse and the boat to stop. I had dark sails.[3]

---

[3] Most racing boats have three basic sails. Between the mast and the bow is the headsail, and between the mast and the stern is the mainsail. For down-wind sailing, most will use a spinnaker, a large, lightweight sail that looks a bit like a parachute. Bigger boats carry several headsails and spinnakers of different sizes and weights, and swap them depending on the wind strength.

The jellyfish came to the lough in swarms, attracted by the free sewage buffet laid on by the authorities in Belfast. Twice a day a sludge-boat chugged to the mouth of the lough with an honour-guard of gulls, dumped its load, and chugged back. The sewage followed it in again on the next tide.

The sewage itself wasn't a problem, so long as you kept your mouth shut if you fell in. But sailing through a patch of jellies slowed you down dramatically. The tiller vibrated in your hand as they thumped against the rudder. I'd never found this problem discussed in any of the sailing books. At absolutely no point in *Swallows and Amazons* does Susan cry, 'John, look out, there's a patch of shit-eating jellyfish ahead!'

On the other hand, a jellyfish was a useful weapon. You could pick one up in a bailing scoop and throw it at the opposition. The scoop worked a bit like a slingshot, and a talented jelly-flinger could achieve remarkable distance and accuracy. I remember, with gratifying clarity, the night when someone landed one on the back of Dobbs's neck. As it slid down the back of his shirt he emitted a girlish scream that echoed round the hills above the Antrim coastline, causing birds to fly squawking into the air, and making golfers in Greenisland hook crucial puts. His reaction surprised me – the jellies didn't sting, not much anyway.

I make it sound as if we were sailing on some sort of sewer. We were, but I'd hate anyone to think less of the place for that. When I first went there, Carrickfergus Sailing Club itself was a Nissen hut, built on steel stilts (somewhat rusted) rising out of the sea behind the eastern wall of Carrickfergus Harbour. In the gents', you could see the sea through the gaps between the (slightly rotten) floorboards. The pool table used to rock in stormy weather.

A year or two after I joined the club, the council built a marina. It was constructed by digging a big hole in the foreshore, and heaping the spoil beside it. Carrickfergus Sailing Club moved to the spoil heap, flattened it out a bit, and built a new clubhouse. The club was less at risk of falling into the sea, but it was beside a coal-yard by the west wall of the harbour, so that the first thing you had to do each time you went sailing was wash the coal-dust off your boat.

I spent a lot of time there. There was racing on Tuesday and Thursday evenings through spring and summer. There were regattas and open meetings on summer weekends, and there was yet more racing on Sundays over the winter, with just a break for December and January. The winter racing was frequently so cold that you had to sail alternating each hand between your thighs to try to keep it warm. It was not always easy to convince yourself you were having fun.

Every July I went to the sailing-school week – I started going even before I got my own boat. The first year was about the very basic things – the way you adjusted (trimmed) the sails depending on what angle to the wind direction you were sailing, or how a boat can't sail straight into the wind, but can only manage a 45-degree angle to it. We learned how to make progress to windward by sailing one way, then tacking to go the other, making a zigzag course like a mountain road that climbs by a series of hairpins. The whole business of getting upwind is called beating, which just about sums up the slog involved.

There were endless tacking drills – as the boat turns through the wind, and the sails fill from the other side, you need to swap from one side of the boat to another. Since in a dinghy your weight is essential to keep the thing upright, you need to time turning the boat and shifting your weight just right. You had to do it on chairs in the clubhouse before they'd let you do it on the lough, calling out 'ready about' to warn your crew, then 'lee-ho', before pushing the tiller (broom handle) to turn the boat and crossing from one chair to the other.

After you mastered tacking, they let you do gybing – the same, but going downwind, so the stern of the boat turns through the wind. It's harder than tacking, because the boat is going faster so you have less control, and the sails don't flap – the wind just switches instantly from one side to the other. This means that if there is much breeze at all, the horizontal boom that holds the foot of the mainsail comes across the boat very fast, very hard, and conveniently situated at head-height. Even in something as pedestrian as a Mirror, you could hurt yourself if you got in the way.

Setting aside the possibility of taking off the top of your head like a boiled egg, the violence involved in gybing makes it a manoeuvre highly prone to going wrong in other ways. After I grew too big for Mirrors, I sailed a single-handed dinghy called a Laser. On windy days my gybing technique was something like 'steer downwind, give the mainsheet a yank to flick the mainsail over the boat, hold my breath, shut my eyes, wait till I surface, and swim back to my capsized boat'.[4]

The traditional advice for safer gybing is to do it when the boat is going as fast as possible, preferably surfing down a wave. The faster you're sailing away from the wind, goes the logic, the less pressure there is on the sails. No doubt if you're Ellen MacArthur, this is a viable piece of advice. For people like me, it's asking that at a moment of maximum terror, with sheets of water flying everywhere and the whole boat vibrating like it's about to erupt, you do the one thing you know is guaranteed to make it even scarier. I don't think so.

Once or twice, sailing school was blighted by strong wind. Then you could spend all week in the classroom, sailing grey plastic stacking-chairs and brooms and looking out of the window at the white-capped waves. I didn't mind. I was hot stuff with a chair and a broom.

On the water, of course, it was rather mixed. It took some time for my reputation to recover from the first time I launched a boat – not *33208*, this one was borrowed – as helmsman. On the narrow slipway, with an offshore breeze, the technique was to float the boat off its trailer pointing shorewards, head to wind, sails flapping. The crew got in. Then the helmsman physically manhandled the boat round to point offshore, and jumped in just as the sails filled and the boat sailed away.

Full of self-importance, I held the boat as my crew – mercifully not Dobbs at this point – got in.

---

[4] The mainsheet is the rope attached to the aft corner of the mainsail, used to adjust the sail's angle to the wind. Headsails and spinnakers have similar sheets, which are also used to switch the sail from one side of the boat to another in a tack. They're the most important sail control you have, and are used almost constantly to make changes to the trim of the sails.

'Ready?' I barked.

'Ready,' said the crew.

'Turning the boat,' I said. I turned the boat. The wind caught the sails. It set off rather faster than I had anticipated. I jumped after it. In my defence, it's hard to jump off a slippery slipway, wearing sodden dinghy boots.

I had missed the boat in the most horribly literal sense. But I got a foot tangled in the mainsheet rope, which had the double effect of yanking me off my feet, and pulling in the mainsail, so the boat accelerated. Still tangled up, I was ignominiously towed out to sea by one foot, flat on my back with seawater going up my nose, ineffectually flapping my arms at the passing sky.

By the time I'd hauled myself on board, all the other members of the sailing school were holding on to each other and howling. Two boats crashed with a splintering of plywood. Still their crews laughed.

If I want an example of how I've matured since I was twelve, well, I am now prepared to concede that this indignity was not totally devoid of some elements of humour. But at the time there were no words available to describe the embarrassment. I compounded things by tearfully shouting back, 'It's not funny! I might have drowned!', thereby acquiring a catchphrase that lasted for my whole dinghy-sailing career.

Racing, though, was what the school was really about. After a year in the beginners' group, I progressed to the racing section of the course. We spent days practising things like starts. Sailing races start against the wind, at an imaginary line, normally between a buoy and a race officer's boat. A gun or a hooter indicates the time till the start – you normally get a ten- or five-minute signal on which to start your watch. The idea is to manage your approach so you hit the line as the watch reaches zero. Meanwhile, everyone else tries to do the same. The instructors used to deliberately set a line that was too short for everyone to fit at once, so you all had to squabble for space. If you got it wrong you ended up behind the others, going slowly in their dirty air, or you got pushed over the line early, and got disqualified. We would spend whole days doing this routine again and again – the gun for one start was the five-minute signal for the next.

Then onto short races – just a mark a few hundred yards upwind of the start, so you zigzagged up to that, rounded it, and ran back downwind to the line you'd started at. Normally there was some requirement about the number of tacks you had to put in on the upwind leg, and the number of gybes coming back. It was a great way to learn about boat handling, and about sailing on a crowded course. There was a constant background of shouting and good-natured abuse. On a sunny summer afternoon, there was nowhere I'd rather have been.

I won my fair share of the starts and the short races. I could do the technical bits of sailing, the bits that involved listening to instructions and putting them into action. Where it all went wrong was when Dobbs and I went out for the longer, more serious evening races. Instead of lasting ten minutes, these lasted for more like an hour and a half. And I just couldn't do it. I couldn't concentrate for that long. I couldn't get the tactics right for dealing with shifts in the wind direction, with the unpredictable tides close inshore, or with keeping out of the wind-shadows created by the other boats. I was forever tacking to get out of one problem, only to sail straight into another one, one that everyone else had seen coming.

I got beaten, again and again. I got beaten by people who had barely learned to sail, because they were able to keep their minds on steering the boat in a straight line, while I was busy trying to remember something I'd once read about how the friction between the wind and the surface of the sea means that the wind direction at the top of the mast is slightly different to the direction at the bottom.

I used to be driven to fury by a guy called Brian, who didn't know the names for any of the ropes, and who had 'port' and 'starboard' written on the relevant sides of his tiller so he knew which was which. Brian could beat me without having to try. Brian could beat me while his crew lay on his back in the bottom of the boat with his arms and legs in the air pretending to be a dog.

One night Brian sailed his scruffy old shed of a boat straight past Dobbs and me, and as he went, called across, 'Pull the doofer-dangle rope there – no . . . no . . . yes, that's the jobbie. About two inches.' I told him, politely, that the rope to which he was referring was properly called the *vang*, and ordered Dobbs to leave it alone. Naturally, Dobbs gave it a pull. Immediately the boat picked up a bit of speed.

Brian was not only a better sailor than me, even if he functioned entirely on instinct, but his good-natured willingness to hand out advice made him a better human being as well. I would have very much enjoyed watching him being struck by lightning.

The club was a kind of home. There was a decent sized group of young sailors, and for the summer months the club was our hangout. When there wasn't any racing, we sometimes went out for the equivalent of a kick-about – picking out our own course among a few of the racing marks. We worked on boats, or more likely mocked someone else's efforts in that department, and we played pool on the table in the clubhouse, lining pairs of ten-pence pieces up on the edge of the table to secure our place in the queue.

Sometimes we sailed on the bigger racing-boats when they were short of crew, especially when stronger winds meant the dinghy racing was cancelled. There were a dozen or more boats from 30–40 feet in length based in the marina, and you could usually find a place if you walked along the pontoons and asked. Occasionally skippers were sufficiently desperate that they'd come over to the dinghy park looking for us, securing our services with a few tins of lager.

The big boats worked the same way as the dinghies, except that everything was scaled up, and the forces involved were rather greater. A jib sheet on a Mirror could be pulled in by a ten-year-old, while on a 40-footer it would have to be handled with a winch. This meant more crew, perhaps ten or twelve, each with a specific job. In tacking 33208, Dobbs could easily look after releasing the jib sheet on one side of the boat and bringing it in on the other. On a big boat the same job required at least three people.

I was rather better at big-boat sailing than I ever was in a dinghy. That's because on a big boat there were jobs that suited me perfectly – technical jobs involving putting up one sail and taking down another, or switching sails from one side to another in a tack or gybe. They demanded very little in the way of talent, just the ability to remember to do a sequence of things in the correct order, and to have enough understanding and imagination to solve any problems that might crop up – a sail ripping or a rope breaking.

I was a good enough crewman to sail at several of the bigger regattas in Ireland, and on boats that quite often won. I was part of a Northern Irish team at a regatta called the European Team Championships, though in truth the event wasn't nearly as prestigious as it sounds. I even managed to get selected for a crew to compete at a televised match-racing series held in Cowes, only to have to pull out because my parents felt that I ought to be worrying about my A levels instead.

On a big boat, the only people who needed sophisticated tactical nous and actual sailing ability were the guys at the back – the helmsman, the tactician and the navigator, known collectively as the afterguard. They decided what the fastest way to get the boat round the course was. They were the stars, the guys who got their names in the papers. The rest of us just helped.

Of course, dinghy sailing was where most afterguard sailors had perfected their skills. That was why, however good I might be at big-boat sailing, however much I might enjoy it, I always went back to bobbing about on the effluent in an 11-foot plywood box with Dobbs. That was the only way I was ever going to get my career up and running. I always remembered the master plan.

In January 2006, the master plan for my comeback was

rather less grandiose. My original idea had been to go back to dinghy racing. I even had a notion of trying to track down Stephen Dobbs, before remembering that I once spent an entire afternoon trying to work out if I could drown him and make it look like an accident. He'd probably changed, but unless he'd had the help of a plastic surgeon and a skilled psychiatrist, he was unlikely to have changed enough.

No. Dinghy racing was tough and competitive, and looked far too much like mediocrity waiting to happen. I wanted to go back to sailing, but not to an exact facsimile of my teenage years. I'd wasted fourteen years away from the sport, so I decided that if I was going to get to the Mediterranean blue-skies dream, I'd better skip ahead a bit, and focus my efforts on crewing bigger boats. Clearly that meant I wouldn't get to stand behind the wheel barking out orders, but I was just going to have to let that bit of the dream go.

So step one was to find someone with a nice big boat who'd take me sailing. Step two was to be so good at it that I got to fulfil the blue-skies, blue-sea professional dream. Having thought about it for a while, I decided to put step two aside for the moment and concentrate on step one.

I really had no idea how to find a skipper. Sailing was a world I'd left behind, and other than going on an expensive sailing course of some sort, there didn't seem to be any easy way back into it. The only thing I could think of was to go to the London Boat Show, simply because that's the traditional place for sailors to get their winter fix of shiny brass portholes and comedy knickers with the international flag-code for 'You may enter harbour' printed on them.

I found it hard to imagine I was going to get talent-spotted as I wandered round the show, but maybe I'd fall into conversation with someone. Maybe . . . well, I didn't know. I knew I was kidding myself. But it seemed a better bet than sitting at home.

A more solid reason for going was that there would be a sneaky chance to see what I could still do. I knew the basic mechanics of sailing wouldn't have slipped away, but I had begun to wonder just how instinctive things would still be. I had assumed it would be April at least, after I got back from Australia, before I could actually go sailing for real. But at the show, just for a little while, I could get back on the water; according to the show website, they were running come-and-try-it sessions using a temporary indoor pool and some fans. It seemed like a good idea to start off the comeback on my own in a glorified toy rather than on someone else's racing-yacht.

The Boat Show was bewildering in its size. There were huge hunks of highly polished fibreglass everywhere, and since they were at eye level, it made the whole thing feel like a shiny-white plastic maze. You couldn't see more than a few yards in any direction; you certainly couldn't see anything that would give you a chance to get your bearings. The bright lights and the noise of at least a dozen competing sound systems made it even more disorientating. After ten minutes my head was spinning from the sensory over-stimulation. Looking at the ceiling helped. It was the only thing I could see that no one was trying to make me buy.

The come-and-try-it pool was in a marquee at the end of a long corridor off the main hall. It took me half the morning to find it. The contrast with the rest of the show was wonderful – the marquee was dimly lit and very quiet, with little reflections from the water dancing across the roof. The pool was rectangular, 80 metres long, with chest-high blue plastic sides. It reminded me of a paddling pool I'd had when I was about six, except on a scale big enough to generate the slightly eerie feeling that goes along with large bodies of very still water. There was a row of giant fans along one side that looked well able to stir up a gale. I found a bored-looking man who told me to sign a disclaimer form that ran to several pages (and which made provision for death or injury as a result of flooding, which seemed unduly pessimistic), and come back in two hours.

When the time came, I and half a dozen others, several of them in business suits, got issued with drysuits that were still clammy from their last occupants, and were each given a small rubber-duck yellow dinghy with pale-blue sails. Someone switched on the fans, which wound up into a low roar and blew dark ripples across the water. I stepped into my dinghy, and an instructor gave it a shove out into the pool.

It was immediately apparent that sailing hadn't much changed. I pulled in the mainsheet, hand over hand, steering casually with a knee against the tiller. I could have done it with my eyes closed – it was barely more conscious than breathing. The dinghy accelerated across the pool.

'Jesus, mate, watch where you're going, will you?'

I was ten seconds into my comeback, and already I'd found a sailing indignity to which I had not previously been subjected. There were instructors, wearing drysuits,

wading around up to their chests in water, manhandling
dinghies in the same helpful spirit as the fairground
employees who reliably spoil all the fun of the dodgems
by leaping on board your dodgem and seizing control. I'd
just fetched one of them a crack about the head with the
bow of my dinghy. He grabbed my boat and turned me
round in a direction I didn't want to go.

I'd sailed into him because I'd had to remove my
glasses. I could sail fine, I just couldn't see where I was
going. It was a bad combination. It struck me that since
I'd always been short-sighted, but never worn glasses on
a boat, my whole sailing career must have been a bit
blurred. I laughed – it seemed silly that I'd never thought
of that before. Maybe I'd have been a better sailor if I'd
been able to see what was going on?

The rest of the tiro yachties were genuine beginners,
who ended up constantly being blown into a heap of
dinghies and masts at the downwind side of the pool
where the drysuit guys tried to untangle them. I, on the
other hand, had the skill required to build up some speed.
And that meant I could hit the things I couldn't see pretty
hard. There were half a dozen guys in the water, and I
think I walloped them all at some point, although
obviously I can't be sure. None of them talked to me
afterwards.

Not being able to see didn't make much difference
anyway, other than to the minor issue of hitting stuff. It's
a point I've made before, and I'll make it again before
we're finished: sailing is all about wind, and you can't see
wind. You have to find something invisible and turn it
into motion.

You can't see wind, but there are clues about what it's

doing. Ripples on the water – on the pool there were dark stripes in front of each fan. How the sails set. Sometimes there are more comedic signs – if you're sailing on an inland lake, it's worth knowing that cows usually stand with their backs to the wind.

But most of all, you can feel it. The differences between good racing sailors and people like me rests on an ability to feel the wind better, or an instinct about what it's going to do next. Things that are so subtle there is no way to explain them. I know there is no way to explain them, because I used to read book after book where gifted sailors tried their best, again and again, to explain how they did what they did, but couldn't come close.

So far as sailing was concerned, I'd learned the grammar, I could spell, I could quote the classics at length, but I couldn't feel the poetry that lay at its heart.

Yet even I could tell that the wind in the pool was peculiar. The breeze from the fans was absolutely nothing like the real thing. It was regular and predictable, even as you passed a fan, rode the gust, and hit the lull. Even at its strongest, it didn't feel right. Real wind is what you feel at the top of a cliff – it has weight, momentum, it's unwilling to bend round you, even if it's only of a moderate strength. It's hard to find real wind on land. The fans produced something that I can only describe as 'fluffy'. I know that sounds silly, but I don't think I can do any better. I was pleased that I could tell the difference – it was a sensitivity I didn't expect to have.

I sailed back and forward in front of the fans, across the wind. Reaching, technically. There wasn't really the space to do anything else. A tack at one end of the pool, and a gybe at the other. In the cavernous tent, with the thundering fans, it was hardly exciting. But it was therapeutic. Just to be sailing again felt good, felt right. When you learn something young, you learn it well. I was still a sailor of some sort. For the first time I was sure I was doing the right thing.

Chapter Three

Princess 61

GOING TO SEA FOR NO BETTER REASON THAN TO ENJOY yourself is something that has always had overtones of wealth and privilege. This is what we might call the 'posh problem'. Non-sailors tend to locate sailing on a continuum that has polo at one end and Bertie Wooster at the other. For the most part, it doesn't matter how hard I try to explain the thrill of surfing down a wave in a strong breeze, or the beauty of a sunrise at sea, the image is of me sitting on deck swigging gin while lots of chaps in white trousers dash about shouting 'splice the mainbrace' and, with a bit of luck, fetching more gin.

Up to this point, I have addressed this issue by looking the other way whenever it has loomed, sticking my fingers in my ears and singing 'A Life On The Ocean Wave' as loudly as I can. This is appropriate, because that's how I dealt with it for probably the first fourteen years of my life. I just didn't realise that was how people saw sailing – like all kids, I grew up with the firm belief that everything that happened in my family was normal,

anything else was a bit deviant. It was unsettling to go
round to a friend's house after school and discover their
washing machine door wasn't wedged shut with a bit of
broom handle and a brick.

Even when everyone else's prejudices started to trickle
into my consciousness, it didn't really make sense. I
wasn't posh, I didn't think. The people I sailed with
weren't posh. Come to think of it, I was a bit foggy on
what 'posh' was, other than a general-purpose insult. But
that was enough – it was an insult, so I knew the term
couldn't possibly describe me.

In truth, I probably was a bit posh, at least in the terms
intended by those bandying the insults. I admit it. I come
from middle-class gin-drinking stock. But that wasn't
really relevant, because what *I* was never really seemed to
be the issue – no one accused me of being posh on my
own merits, it was only on the basis that I went sailing at
the weekend. It seemed like a standardised response, just
as anyone who'd admitted to having a horse would have
been similarly slurred, even if it was an undistinguished
nag living on a diet of thistles on a local farm.

What it took me quite a long time to figure out was that
there was a difference between demographics and personal
circumstances. For a start, Northern Ireland wasn't then,
and still isn't really, stratified by class. Matters of class are
swamped by religion and politics. For another, even on
those terms Carrickfergus was not a posh club – sailors
from such hotbeds of proletarian activism as the Royal
Ulster Yacht Club were fond of referring to it (not without
affection) as 'Carrickfergus Working Men's Club'.

I can't remember the background of most of the
members. Most of the junior Mirror sailors failed to live

up to the over-privileged stereotype – they paid for their sailing with Saturday jobs, and anyone who showed up with anything as swish as a new suit of sails was immediately engulfed in a hail of jellyfish. A new suit of sails cost something approaching £200, so it didn't happen very often.

The bigger boats owned by the senior members demanded more money, but usually it came from mundane sources. There was a guy who owned a TV shop; I remember that mainly because of my mother's rather quaintly referring to it as a 'wireless shop'. There were several who worked for the local council. There was the expected contingent of dentists and doctors, accountants and estate agents. There was a cowboy electrician, who left a string of small fires and falsified VAT numbers across Northern Ireland and most of Scotland. And at the less mundane end of the spectrum there was Uncle Norman, a one-man warning about the perils of stereotyping.

Uncle Norman was not, so far as I know, anyone's uncle, but that's what everyone called him. He was ruddy-faced, extravagantly moustached and of late middle-age, and was an alternately affable or irascible presence through most of my teenage sailing. I'll be honest – he scared me. In an evening race, he was quite capable of using his 35-foot boat to try to ram Dobbs and me because he didn't like juniors in dinghies, and without the slightest acknowledgement of the incident, slipping me a stealthy gin in the bar, on the basis that the younger you start the more you can drink. He never actually slipped me a tonic to go with it, which meant my early gin-drinking career made my hair stand on end as my scalp clenched. It helped if you ate the lemon.

Uncle Norman was a hard-drinking, hard-living (a roll of drums would not be over the top here . . .) ladies' hairdresser. Apparently, in the 1970s, he had been the coiffeur of choice for fashionable Belfast. My mother still recounts the story of Uncle Norman cutting her hair – the only occasion on which this was allowed to happen. When Dad arrived to pick her up, Norman parked her under a dryer for two hours while he and Dad went to the bar across the road. It was one of our family's little mysteries that this was lovable behaviour from Norman, and despicable behaviour from Dad. Mum said it was the worst haircut she ever had. I didn't argue, except to point out that really it was only half a haircut. That was the whole problem. But even she had to admit that her hair was really, really dry.

Uncle Norman had a string of incidents involving drink-driving that, in the Northern Ireland of the 1980s, was regarded as an occupational hazard of being a gregarious gentleman with an active social life. He once barrelled off a motorway via the embankment and, landing in someone's garden, extricated himself from the wreckage and walked the two miles home. He didn't report this to anyone, presumably hoping that the owners of the garden wouldn't notice a Triumph TR6 upside down on the lawn and a set of muddy footprints zigzagging towards Antrim. In particular, he hoped not to attract, yet again, the attentions of the police. By the time I was aware of him, his licence was a fond memory.

He sailed instead – sometimes racing, sometimes cruising. Though Uncle Norman's idea of cruising was to load up his boat with a few drinking mates and head off for a few days. These trips were legendary – many who fancied themselves hardened imbibers were returned as pale, confused husks of their former selves. No one ever seemed to know where it was they'd been. It can only have been Scotland or the Isle of Man, but no witnesses ever saw them. It was as if Uncle Norman had sailed them into another dimension.

Not that Norman couldn't quaff and coif at the same time. He carried his scissors everywhere, and used to cut hair in pubs. I'd rather have sailed round the world slowly with Stephen Dobbs than have Uncle Norman cut my hair in a pub. Apparently, his best work was just before he went glassy eyed and the scissors slipped from his fingers to land quivering, point-down in the wood of your bar stool, just between your thighs.

Uncle Norman was no one's idea of a 'typical' sailor. He was no one's idea of a typical anything. And this is the point. None of the sailors I met when I was a kid, and I met a lot, were anyone's idea of a typical sailor. I never recognised any of the stereotypes, because there were too many individuals, and they were all different. Poshness was neither here nor there.

The first cracks in this complacency appeared shortly after I arrived at college in Durham, within a few days of my giving up sailing anyway. I went to the sailing club's stall at the societies' fair.

'You sail? But you're, like, Scottish or something?' said the girl behind the desk, who according to a badge was called Henrietta. She turned round to talk to one of the other members on the stall: 'James, this chap's Scottish. They don't have sailing in Scotland, do they?' It was as if the laws of physics stopped at the Hampshire border.

James flicked his fringe out of his eyes, and said, 'Well,

they do, but they don't have much money up there, so it's not like it is on the Solent.'

James asked me what school I'd gone to. I told him. He laughed, and said he'd never heard of it. He explained that most of the better sailors came from the better schools, which meant there wasn't much point in my coming for a team try-out since I clearly wasn't going to be good enough.

James and Henrietta weren't representative of anything, possibly not even of the sailing club. I wouldn't know, because I didn't join. But the posh problem began to make some sort of sense. They were posh, and they knew it; the unexpected twist was they quite liked it. This possibility had never even occurred to me. For them, it was a system that meant that in their velvet-lined journey through life they would meet only arseholes just like themselves. They didn't want to go sailing with me because I hadn't been to the right school; I didn't want to go sailing with them, and for exactly the same reason. If I'd been a little less insecure, I'd have recognised it immediately as a win-win situation.

As it was, I was left angry by the encounter. I felt small. It was the first time I'd come across that kind of snobbery, and I wasn't prepared for it. I was frustrated to think that a shared sport might lead people to conclude I had anything in common with James and Henrietta, but of course that's exactly what they would do. That's how the world works: that's how you build a stereotype. I still reckoned people like them were in a minority; unfortunately, it was a very noisy minority. Most of us weren't like that at all. At least, I didn't think so.

But even if I was right about all that, I would have had

to admit that my socialist theory of yachting was not helped by the most visible bits of sailing always having been the most exclusive – the America's Cup, the expensive yachts belonging to people like Simon le Bon, or the over-privileged splashing about of most of Europe's royal families. That was what grabbed the headlines, even in most of the specialist press. That was something I tried hard to ignore. There were rather too few stories of kids fighting their way out of the ghetto with a dinghy and a dream, but all the same, that wasn't my fault. That was the kids in the ghetto's fault. They could do it if they wanted it enough.

I clung doggedly to my egalitarian view for the next fourteen years. I tried not to notice as strings of well-spoken young men and women won sackfuls of Olympic medals. I applauded as Ellen MacArthur, armed with a dinghy and a dream, fought her way out of a reasonably nice bit of Derbyshire.

When I came back to the sailing world, the whole posh issue was one of the things on my mind. I was older, less confident in my opinions, and less of a sailor. By the time I arrived at the 2006 Boat Show, I could face the possibility of sailing being posh if that was what the evidence suggested, because it was so long since I'd been on a boat that I would no longer be implicated.

I kept eyeing the crowds, looking for clues. Who were they? Where had they come from? Excuse me, did you go to public school? Are you posh? Are you like me? Are you the King of Sweden?

Of course, I could tell damn all. They'd all left the Bentley at home, and they weren't wearing tabards with their socio-economic grouping written on them. They looked just the same as the crowd who'd been at the previous autumn's bike show in the same venue – a little older maybe, a little less trim, but with the same outdoors look, penchant for fleeces, and obvious interest in spending money.

Even then I knew the Boat Show was probably the wrong place to look – it was just the first chance I got. The demographic there is a bit muddied. While there are a lot of hard-core sailors, who flock to the show to have a drink with their mates in the off-season and make plans for the coming year, or poke about the stands for new bits and pieces, there are also a lot of non-sailors, just there for a look around. That makes the posh problem harder to analyse in the sense of who goes sailing, but the fact that the non-sailors come in the first place casts some light on what the non-sailing world thinks of it all, and how it comes to think it.

Before I went to the show, I found it hard to believe that anyone who wasn't a sailor of some sort would flog their way to London's Docklands on a wet January morning when they could just as well stay at home with a copy of *Boat International* ('The number-one magazine for the global super-yacht industry').[5]

When I was there, I understood. The lifestyle offered by some of the exhibitors was intoxicating. While I was waiting my turn in the come-and-try-it dinghy, I queued up for ten minutes to put a pair of giant felt socks over my shoes and look round a Princess 61-foot powerboat. From

---

[5] It even publishes a yacht interiors supplement: 'Every year owners and their wives spend millions refitting and designing the interiors of the world's finest new builds.' I want to marry a super-yacht owner too.

the outside it was an absurdly swishy chunk of polished fibreglass with aggressive 'go-faster' lines, like a space rocket crossed with a racing car and scaled up a hundred times. Inside, it was all honey-coloured veneers, suede wallpaper and nicely rounded corners on the fitted furniture, like a bachelor pad designed by Fisher-Price. It had all the understated elegance of a fat, middle-aged man driving an open-topped Lamborghini down the King's Road.

I might make fun of it, but I very much liked the idea of diving off the stern swimming-platform into a warm turquoise sea while the boat bobbed at anchor in, let's say, the Bahamas. That's an awful admission for a sailor (rather than a powerboater) to make, so I need to sneer some more at the phallic excesses of the exterior. But, then again, if I was inside it, I wouldn't have to look at that. And I'm sure the suede wallpaper is optional. But it's . . . Arrghh! I don't know.

What was very clear was that I was never going to be rich enough to buy such a boat. I was hard pressed to imagine that any single one of the hundreds of people marching through it in their giant socks were ever going to buy one. It's a world of privilege and conspicuous consumption that borders on the offensive. It's not remotely representative of reality, but it's sure as hell what you remember when you're eating your sandwiches on the train home.

Whatever prejudices non-sailors hold about sailors, they're mild compared to the factionalism that exists within the maritime world. For a start, most of the sailors are very rude about the non-sailors at the show – 'tourists', 'fantasists', 'wannabes'. This is not so much snobbishness as reflex. Most of those who go to sea are fuelled by boiling hostility to everyone else out there. The sailors, like me, hate powerboaters, who they see as noisy and boorish. Every marina in the country seems to be full of expensive powerboats that never go anywhere.

The powerboaters, for their part, can't see why you'd want to spend your weekends bobbing about at the mercy of the wind, and just generally getting in everyone's way, so they hate the sailors. Then they put the throttles down, and head for the Channel Islands for a spot of lunch.

Even the racing sailors and the cruising sailors aren't really very sure about each other, but since they're standing back-to-back surrounded by gun-toting powerboaters, they try to rub along.

The various navies, the fishermen, and everyone else who goes to sea for a living hate the whole bloody lot of them – hence the term WAFI: wind-assisted fucking idiot. There is something about all that natural beauty that really brings out the bastard in everyone.

A few weeks after the Boat Show, on a dark, wet February night, I arrived at Chelsea Football Club. This was a big step forward in my comeback. I had invited myself to a party. I discovered the website of the Royal Ocean Racing Club (not posh, not posh, la, la, la), and found a sort of lonely-hearts for yachties service: a list of boats seeking crew, and a reciprocal list of lonely sailors looking for friends.

The first list varied from the sober, 'Competitive team planning a serious offshore season, looking for experienced bowman and mainsheet trimmer', to the regrettably wacky, 'Work hard, play hard, woooo! We are the mushrooms – the wild fun guys! Come and join the party!!' Would you put your life in the hands of the man who wrote that?

The second list, the lonely sailors, had a different feel. The entries were more self-conscious, and divided sharply along sex lines. The men's entries said things like, 'I'm a talented racing sailor, with 2,000 miles experience as a headsail trimmer, 1,000 miles as a main trimmer. Also a first-class helmsman. Former Olympic weightlifter, and a skilled electronics engineer. First-aid cert, radio cert, Yachtmaster theory exam passed, looking for main-trimming position/second helmsman on a *serious boat only* for the coming season. I hate finishing second, so if you're not planning to win, don't get in touch.' Testosterone leached out of my computer's screen and dripped onto my desk.

Women's entries were more likely to say, 'Just back from my first sailing experience on holiday in Greece and keen to do more – happy to do anything from bottle-washing upwards!!'

I put up an entry: 'Experienced dinghy and big-boat sailor; I've been out of the sport for a few years. Able to fill most positions reasonably, but most familiar with bow. Not available until after the Commonwealth Games.' You see how I combined modesty with that Commonwealth Games teaser? I ought to say that there is no sailing at the Commonwealths, so I wasn't trying to produce an inflated sense of my own competence, just give myself an air of exoticism.

And there was an open invitation to a party at Chelsea FC. Essentially a hiring fair with canapés, the idea was to put lots of skippers in search of crew in the same room as lots of sailors looking for a skipper, and see what might come to pass. I signed up immediately.

That was how, a fortnight later, I found myself wearing a badge that identified me as a man with no friends, trapped in conversation with a man in a blazer and cravat who'd apparently just arrived from 1975. 'Only four rules on my boat, easy to remember, all begin with B: no Birds, Booze, Blasphemy or Buggery. At least not while we're at sea. Do what you like in port.' He roared with laughter. I told him that all seemed jolly reasonable, and edged away.

The nature of the function at least made it easy to start conversations. And I could still speak fluent yachtie, which was a relief. I was able to trade stories of epic gear breakage, and of long, miserable offshore races where we finished with nothing to eat or drink apart from custard powder and a few rusty tins of Tennent's lager.

This ability to talk sailing was essential. Luckily, on the Fulham Road, it was safe to lay it on thick. All the same, there were several wannabe crew members who were quickly sidelined because their sailing experience was limited to something like a Greek flotilla holiday, and they didn't compensate by telling potential skippers about an epic solo transatlantic crossing, cut and pasted out of Francis Chichester's autobiography and onto their own CVs. It's what the rest of us were doing.

With the booze and buggery man safely in a far corner of the room, I started talking to a middle-aged woman looking for crew, and a man about my own age. At the point where I butted in, he was telling her that he was a teacher, and that he'd never heard of a teacher who sailed. When he asked me what I did, I said, deliberately ambiguous, that I was a cyclist. Usually people assumed I was a courier. The woman nodded enthusiastically.

'Ya, ya. Of course,' she said. 'All kinds of people sail these days. On our boat alone we have a solicitor, a surgeon, two City bankers, a hedge fund manager and a high court judge.'

I went to buy myself a drink, and have a long hard think about the 'sailing isn't posh' hypothesis. The room was full of well-dressed people with nice accents. Overheard conversations suggested that total strangers were rapidly finding friends in common. Apart from the teacher and me, everyone seemed to work in the City. I had to admit that the thesis was under some strain.

It took an age to get served. It reminded me of the sailing club bars where, as soon as I had grown enough that my eyes were above counter level, Dad dispatched me to buy drinks so that no one at the table had to leave the conversation. Sometimes I stood there in the press of customers for what felt like hours, a blond fringe and a pair of resigned-looking eyeballs peering at the barman round the ice bucket. The upside was that I was rarely asked for change when I returned to the table. As long as I walked smoothly enough not to jangle and attract attention, I could get rich.[6]

As I waited, a woman approached me, and said, 'You look like a bowman.' I replied that I was. I wasn't surprised she'd picked me out – bowmen tend to be the weediest-looking members of the crew, so any cyclist would look about right. 'This is Mike, our skipper,' she said, indicating a bearded, nautical-looking man who had

---

[6] Never once did a barman, when he'd finally seen me, baulk at the thought of handing a ten-year-old six pints of Smithwick's and a Coke. Happy times.

approached me from the other side. 'I'm Helen. Sorry about the pincer movement, we didn't want you to get away.'

The 45-foot boat they were recruiting for was still being built – they showed me a picture of a sister ship, foaming along under a blue, Mediterranean sky. The boat didn't belong to either of them, but to a man who hadn't been able to make the party because he was off earning the money to pay for the boat.

'Mac's our owner,' said Helen. 'He's a most marvellous owner too, we're very lucky.' Just the tiniest bit like a sentence that should come from a sheepdog, but otherwise she and Mike seemed relatively normal.

Given that the only thing they knew about my sailing skill was that I looked about right, they seemed surprisingly keen, perhaps a little worryingly so. But we talked about what their season's aims were, what I'd done in the past, and just generally seemed to get on. They were planning to do Cowes Week, which was one of the events I wanted to do, and their big target for the season was the offshore race from Cowes to La Rochelle, that season's longest event. Again, it was on my to-do list.

Helen explained excitedly that their owner had a flat that was the very finest place to watch the fireworks display on the Friday of Cowes Week. I can't stand fireworks (something to do with a Northern Irish upbringing and an entirely rational fear of loud bangs, perhaps), but we were getting on so well that I thought I'd better not mention it.

I didn't get the impression that Helen and Mike were really a force to be reckoned with in the world of significant yacht races. I'd love to say that impression was an old salt's instinctive insight into their personalities.

Actually, there was a list of slightly mediocre results on the back of the picture of the boat. But I wanted to start somewhere manageable – so far, all I knew about my return to sailing was that I could sail a glorified rubber duck up and down a swimming pool in a tent. Helen and Mike were probably fuelled by enthusiasm rather than genius, and that suited me perfectly. We agreed that they'd get in touch when the boat had arrived, by which point I'd be back from the Commonwealths, and ready for a spot of retirement.

I took the bus home (thereby becoming perhaps the first person in history to catch a bus home from a Royal Ocean Racing Club party; the invitation had said 'barges at midnight', but I didn't have a barge). I congratulated myself on having found a starting point, one that was probably not so very far from where I'd left off. I had expected it to be quite difficult to get back into a rather insular sport – yet all it had required was a poke about on the internet, and the ability not to disgrace myself at a social gathering.

Of course, all I had was a promise, but I was fairly confident it would work out. And if it didn't, well, there had been dozens of people in the room, half of them looking for crew, and the other half a group who, a few conversations had revealed, could in large number be filed under 'wildly inexperienced' or 'testosterone-charged danger to shipping'. I managed to be neither (you should have seen some of these people), so it seemed likely that someone would take me sailing. I could still talk the talk, so the chances were they'd keep taking me sailing, since I'd easily be able to shift the blame for any disasters I caused onto someone else.

53

The only thing about all this was that it hadn't been much of a challenge, which was nice, in a way, but left me feeling a bit deflated, like I'd got myself all psyched up for a fight that hadn't happened. I hadn't realised how much I'd been concentrating on the question of how to get started – I was like an athlete who focuses so hard on the selection trials that when they're selected they don't know what to do.

I wiped myself a porthole on the steamed-up window of the bus and peered out at the rain. I couldn't believe how depressed easy success was making me – after all, I'd got what I wanted. The bus sat in stationary traffic, and a hen party in pink tutus sprinted past, trying to get into the dry. As I looked out at them, I thought of my Mediterranean dream. I'd taken a very big step in the right direction. My mood lightened; I started to smile. Suddenly anything seemed possible.

First, at just the point where the sailing season was getting underway, I had the Commonwealth Games to deal with. Five weeks in Melbourne, in February–March, had its compensations. The weather was fine, and if I rode my bike out of Melbourne past St Kilda and on down the shoreline of Port Phillip Bay I could see sailing boats – sometimes what appeared to be hundreds of them – out on the sparkling water. I watched with an expert eye – an expert eye that might, as things turned out, have been better employed in looking where I was going. But it didn't really matter; the damage to me was slight, and the dog was pretty elderly anyway.

I landed back at Heathrow early on a wet Wednesday morning at the end of March, worrying about how I was going to get home with a pile of bikes and equipment that had broken the record for 'greatest quantity of luggage checked onto a Qantas flight by an economy passenger'.[7]

I'd been away from home and living a different life for long enough that the rush-hour journey into London was unfamiliar and a bit disorientating. I was jetlagged, tired, and when I finally got home I just wanted to go to bed, but instead I had almost immediately to go to a meeting at my publishers' where my only contribution was to say 'whatever you think' to every question I was asked. It was, quite sincerely, the best I could do.

While I was there I got a text message. It just said, 'Really need crew 4 this w.end – can u come? Please, please. Beth.' It was a surprise – I'd managed to forget the whole sailing project almost completely. It felt like months since I'd been at the RORC party; by the time I'd got through my races at the Games even my training rides along the beach seemed a long time ago.

I didn't recognise the phone number, or have any idea who Beth was. I just texted back, 'OK, where and when?'

---

[7] 85kg, to be exact. I had three bikes, for a start, plus four sets of wheels and any amount of other stuff. It took up three airport trolleys. On the way out I received an offer of assistance from a barbershop quartet in straw-boaters and striped blazer costume, which was pleasingly odd. On the way back, Qantas lessened the difficulty of my arrival in London by sending most of my stuff to Los Angeles.

Chapter Four

Afterglow

ONLY A LITTLE MORE THAN FORTY-EIGHT HOURS after arriving back from Australia, and still in a personal time-zone that was somewhere around Thailand, I caught a train to Southampton. I found Beth – 'wearing a bright red jacket' (she wasn't wrong there) – sitting in the back carriage, as promised.

'Have a beer,' she said, rummaging in a holdall between her feet and tossing me a can. 'This is Anne,' she continued, introducing me to the woman on her left. 'She's a bridesmaid.' It was pleasing that things had taken a turn for the surreal so soon.

Apparently Beth had had to organise a hen weekend, which had clashed with a weekend's sailing. Rather than miss sailing, she'd decided to have the party in Southampton, so she could do both. As she explained, all she had to do was ensure that everyone else was sufficiently hungover on Saturday and Sunday mornings that they wouldn't notice she'd gone.

From the little I knew about the town, it was clear that

taking a hen weekend to Southampton would almost certainly result in her losing several friends, and having her invitation to the wedding angrily revoked. She can't possibly have not known this. I'd been back in sailing for approximately thirty seconds, and already I'd met someone who shared my adolescent sense of perspective on the matter.

The train trip was fun. Beth and Anne were friendly, and they had that Friday air of two people escaping the office to do something dramatically different. Beth was enjoyably chaotic – after inadvertently dropping most of the contents of her handbag onto the floor while looking for her ringing phone, she took the call while using extravagant gestures to signal her appreciation of the various strangers who picked everything up for her. Then she told me what she and Chris and Brian had got up to the previous weekend during the Warsash Series. My not knowing who Chris or Brian were, or what the Warsash Series might be, only made this feel more welcoming.

When we got to Southampton my new friend abandoned me in a pub with a group of men in matching crew-jackets – yachties are fond of matching kit, like kids at English-language summer schools. All conversation was swamped by the noise of a local band pretending they were headlining Glastonbury. We spent the evening grinning at each other, and since we didn't waste time talking we had far, far too much to drink. Sometime after midnight I got taken to someone's house, and spent the night on a sofa, with my head spinning.

I slept badly, partly because I'd got pissed for the first time in six months, but mainly because I was nervous.

That was nothing new. A career as an athlete meant I had been nervous about something or other continuously since 1999. As a result I could identify this immediately as the very worst kind of nervousness – the *shit sans frontiers* kind, where you have no idea whatsoever about what's going to happen. None. Like the first time I ever kissed a girl, aware that the reaction could be anything from reciprocation to the police being called. (I got complete indifference – a triumph, I reckoned at the time.)

It wasn't the sailing that worried me per se. I knew from the previous evening's train trip that Beth had been pretty desperate when she contacted me originally (she'd got my details off the RORC register), and that not much in the way of competence was expected from me. Sitting still and not getting in the way would do.

It was that I just didn't know how I was going to feel about it all. This is not the kind of thing I usually worry about. It isn't that I'm not emotional, or that I'm not in touch with those emotions, it's more that I don't pay them very much attention. I learned early in life that looking happy led people like my parents to snap, 'What are you looking so happy about?' Looking unhappy got you, 'Cheer up – it might never happen.'

Lest it sound like I'm slinking off into the murky, if lucrative, world of the misery memoir, in the 1980s everyone's parents were like this. A father who uttered the phrase, 'Is something the matter? Is something wrong at school?' would have been hauled before a social worker and accused of trying to raise a homosexual. If you got roughed up at the bus stop and complained about it, the best you were likely to get was, 'Did you not think of hitting him back?'

In the end, I didn't get long to dwell on the tremendously important issue of how I felt. The race had an early start, and we'd all overslept. We needed to leave half an hour ago. And anyway, I had a hangover that, as soon as I sat up on the sofa I'd been sleeping on, became a more pressing concern. Someone found me a pair of old rubber sailing boots that were about six sizes too big, and I clomped off towards the marina with the rest of the crew.

I hung back a bit – I felt awkward not being part of a group who seemed to know each other well. They were long past noticing each other's eccentricities, like Will, who wore electric-blue thermal leggings with shorts and sailing boots, and clearly felt this was an acceptable way to be seen in public. Strangers in the street stopped to stare at him. Most of the strangers looked like they were on their way to an Ellen MacArthur theme party. We grabbed a coffee and a bacon sandwich at a shop near the boat. I don't really like bacon sandwiches, but I bought one anyway to try to fit in. Maybe the coffee would stop my head throbbing.

Cup in one hand, sandwich in the other, we walked across a concrete hard-standing with boats sitting in cradles and on trailers, and down a ramp onto the marina pontoons. There were sailors hurrying back and forth along the pontoons with garden-centre-style trolleys full of bagged-up sails and tools, trying to get heavy items off boats before going racing, and making sure that, since it was windy, all the smaller sails were on board. The breeze, about 25 knots I reckoned, meant that all around was the characteristic slap-slap-slap of halyards against masts. Crews were casting off mooring lines, easing boats out of berths, and motoring out towards the sea.

Our boat, *Afterglow*, was moored on a pontoon at the furthest end of the marina. She was 40 feet long, white, with a thin black stripe on her side. I grabbed a bit of the rigging, hopped lightly over the wire life-lines that ran round the perimeter of the boat, and up onto the deck. Just the way I used to do it. It was hard to believe how long I'd been away. There was a request from Dougal, the skipper, to keep moving, since we were late, so I headed straight down the main companionway hatch to stow my bag.

Down below was strikingly untidy. Coils of rope hung off the low cabin roof, and there was a fair selection of oilskins hanging up to dry alongside them.[8] It was dark and gloomy. Going forwards was like inching through a jungle. But it was the smell that stopped me dead. This racing-yacht smelled of racing-yacht. I'd forgotten there was even a racing-yacht smell, or, more likely, I'd never noticed it because it had always been there. It was damp and slightly acidic, with a little hint of diesel. It grabbed me by the hair like Mr Atkins the French teacher, and yanked me straight back to childhood.

For a fleeting moment I felt everything there was to feel about being twelve years old. My school lunchbox flashed past – an entirely unremarkable bit of Tupperware but apparently very important to my subconscious – followed by the chill of having to get up way before dawn on a winter Monday morning in a cold house to catch the bus for an hour-long trip to school. I have the feeling that when the end is near and my life flashes before my eyes,

---

[8] Most sailors still refer to foul-weather gear as oilskins, despite it being something like sixty years since synthetic fabrics took over from oiled canvas. Oiled canvas wasn't waterproof, but the smell took your mind off how wet you were.

a lunchbox, a dark country road and the rest of a dinghy fleet heading for the horizon are all I'm going to get to represent the 1980s. Just for a moment they weren't things remembered, they were things felt.

It was a more powerful reaction than I had been prepared for. I was still blinking in shock a few moments later when Beth came down the companionway.

'Yeah,' she said, 'it needs a tidy.'

I stowed my bag, put on some oilskins, and went back on deck. It all felt astonishingly normal, to the extent that I didn't really think about it. We cast off, motored out of the marina, and down the river towards the Solent.

Beyond the shelter of the shore there were a lot of white-capped waves, and the sea was a cold-looking grey. The wind was strong, and blew with a solid consistency. It was hard to hear a shout from one end of the boat to the other. When Dougal pointed the boat's bow upwind so we could hoist the mainsail, it pitched hard.

I didn't really do anything to help. I'd avoided over-selling my ability, and the rest of the crew had taken this at even less than its face value and assumed that my highly modest claims were gross exaggerations. I just got bossed about. 'Sit there!' 'Move there!' 'Hold on!' 'Try not to fall overboard!' I think they were enjoying it.

The headsail was brought on deck in a 12-foot-long bag shaped like a sausage, and dragged forward to the bow where a soaking-wet bowman connected it up as water was punched up around him. The sail was hoisted, and the engine killed. Immediately the boat's motion was easier, as it sailed in some sort of harmony with the elements rather than motored against them.

The race was from a starting-line just off Cowes, on

the other side of the Solent, to the Nab Tower, and back. Most races are rather more complicated, involving half a dozen marks or more.[9] To further idiot-proof this one, the only mark of the course was 29 metres tall.

Marks are more usually buoys. Most of the dinghy marks at Carrickfergus were more elusive even than that: they were translucent one-gallon plastic cans, with numbers written on with a marker pen, on a rope tied to a brick. Not only were they hard to see, but because they weren't properly anchored, if it was windy the bastards would move. More than once we all sailed to where we expected to find a mark, and found no sign whatever. Normally we agreed among ourselves to just forget about it. Occasionally, visiting sailors seemed to think this was a little odd. Without my glasses on I was half blind anyway. Just how I ever found these things, even if they didn't move, is a mystery to me.

Race officers are always delighted to send you round whatever else they can find. It appeals to their instinct for the picturesque. Big-boat races from Belfast Lough were often sent round Ailsa Craig, a lump of rock off the Ayrshire coast most notable for giving Peter Alliss something to talk about at Royal Troon Golf Club when finally even he decides there is too much golf on telly.

On Lough Neagh, just off Antrim, they used the Firing Head, a derelict torpedo-testing platform from the Second World War. I was about twenty-five before I realised they had fired the torpedoes out into the lough – as a kid I'd assumed that they'd been fired at Antrim, accepting this as

[9] Although some big races are simple. The instructions for the Round Ireland race state that you start in Wicklow, leave Ireland to starboard, and finish in Wicklow. Sailing round the world isn't a blindingly complex idea either.

an explanation for its rather dog-eared civic appearance. The platform was fairly big, and, in a Mirror, rounding it took quite a while. This gave its extensive bird population plenty of time to crap all over you.

The Nab Tower, off the east coast of the Isle of Wight, is a steel tower on a massive concrete base, originally built during the First World War. (It was designed for catching submarines – the idea was to place several of them in the Straits of Dover and string a net between them. I wouldn't want to cast doubt on the effectiveness of this scheme, but if Wile E. Coyote was trying to catch a submarine, that's how he'd do it.) By the end of the war only two towers had been finished, at the then breathtaking cost of £2 million, and they were both still in Shoreham Harbour. And there they sat.

When the Nab lightship needed replacing a few years later, they towed out one of the towers and sank it in position. The other was quietly dismantled, no doubt to the relief of the dolt who'd designed it six feet too big to get out of the harbour mouth.

The leg out to the tower was downwind. As the starting-gun went, brightly coloured spinnakers were hoisted and the fleet of twenty or so boats headed off down the eastern Solent. From the shore, if you ignored the low, grey skies, the oil refinery at Fawley, and a rusty container ship that happened to be passing, it must have looked rather attractive.

I found that I was still a sailor. I could feel how the wind in the sails and the hull in the water were interacting, how the boat was moving, which way it was going to rock or roll next. I could keep my balance as well as anyone else on board. The strong breeze made it an exciting sail – we were hitting over fifteen knots as we surfed down waves, which doesn't sound dizzying, but it's a lot for a moderately sized, heavyish race boat. There was a roar of water passing, and a clean flat wake behind us.

Downwind sailing in a breeze is a little dangerous. It's not the moon landings, but if you're in the wrong place, or something breaks, it can be bad news. Bear in mind that the boat weighed six tons, plus eleven of us (most of another ton), and that meant there was nearly seven tons of water to push out of the way, and hence a serious load on the rig and sails. The sheets felt more like rods than ropes. On big boats – probably bigger than *Afterglow* – it can be fatally bad news. If you're smart, you keep away from straining bits of deck hardware in case they break in a shower of shrapnel, and let a loaded rope lash free.

I've always loved the teamwork involved in sailing a racing-boat – there were eleven of us on board, and we all had a job. Dougal was behind a wheel about five feet in diameter, concentrating hard. Steering a sailing boat is more complicated than steering almost anything else. It's not about going in a straight line. How you use the rudder is the most important part of the speed equation. You need to steer through waves to maximise speed. You need to be sensitive to the trim of the sails, and to gusts and lulls in the wind. You need to reconcile all this with going in more or less the direction of the next mark. Not an easy job in a breeze – boats sometimes have their own very clear ideas of where they want to go.

If the helmsman gets it wrong, the boat corkscrews out of control into a broach, where the wind overpowers it, leaving it pinned on its side with the mast almost horizontal, and the deck nearly vertical. A lot like a capsize, yes. Except that a boat with a keel will eventually roll back upright of its own accord.

Beth was trimming the spinnaker — standing on the deck watching the sail, easing the sheet out, or pulling it in by calling 'grind!' to Will, who was manning the sheet-winch. He would grind the rope in until Beth called 'OK!' Or more often didn't: 'Beth, for God's sake, tell me when to stop — I'm not doing this for fun.' Grinders and trimmers have been having this discussion since the Polynesians first stuck a mast on a raft.

We had a navigator, armed with an electronic gizmo, closely related to a car sat-nav, who kept making wonderfully authoritative pronouncements. 'Mark at 8 miles, bearing 135 degrees, current course over ground 140 degrees. Time to mark, forty minutes.' I kept waiting for him to give the gizmo a shake, and say, 'It says to turn round as soon as possible.'

Compare and contrast with Dobbs and me bobbing about on Belfast's effluent looking for a one-gallon plastic can: 'Dobbs, can you see the mark?'

'Yes.'

'Where is it?'

'It's your boat, fucking find it yourself.'

This had a military air about it — a tight team, each doing a different job, working in harmony. All over the boat, people tended to winches and held tactical discussions, and generally concentrated. There was a little general chat, but most of the conversation was focused on the sailing. It didn't matter much to me that so far my role could have been played by a bag of potatoes. It was good, really good, to be in the midst of this again.

'Grind!'

'Pole back.'

'Downhaul off. Pole coming back.'

'You're about eight degrees high of the mark.'

'OK – coming down a little. We're pretty deep here, guys. Vang on.'

'Vang on.'

Contrary to what you would expect, boats don't like going straight downwind. It's easy for things to get unbalanced, and then the boat starts to roll from side to side. As the boat rolls, it becomes harder and harder to steer, which is unfortunate, since the only way to damp down the roll is to steer the boat so it is sort of under the sails (wherever the sails want to go is fine – this is not the moment for worrying about the course to the mark). This scenario is known, with only moderate hyperbole, as a death roll.

I mention the term now, because it is about to become highly relevant. 'Coming down a little' was the key phrase. Almost as soon as Dougal had said it, he headed more directly downwind, and the boat rolled to windward. Then to leeward. It came in slow motion. Three or four rolls, and Dougal lost it totally. This death roll finished with the real two-and-a-half-somersaults-with-full-twist-in-the-pike-position of broaches as the boat slewed downwind into the uncontrolled, horribly violent scenario called a Chinese gybe. The boom crashed across the boat, and *Afterglow* was flung on its side.

I clung to a winch on the shuddering vertical deck. I was surrounded by other crew doing the same thing, dangling off whatever they'd been able to grab. I could see Dougal, whose relationship with his boat vis-à-vis who was steering whom had begun to unravel some moments previously, hanging ineffectually off the wheel. By now the masthead was just a few feet away from the water, and the rudder was well clear of it.

'Holy shit!' shouted someone.

Me? I wasn't overly concerned. I'd clung to a lot of decks in my time. The very last big-boat regatta I'd done before my retirement had ended just like this, except that that time we broke the boom. I knew that the dangerous bit of a Chinese gybe is over before you really know what's happening. On this occasion, by the point where I was hanging on ('for dear life', I suppose), it was pretty clear there was no major damage, no one was hurt, and all we had to do was wait for the boat to roll back upright, tidy up the sails and tangled lines, and get on our way. This time we'd been lucky.

Sailing is the only thing I've ever done where in properly scary moments, I stay detached and calm. And trust me, I have very little general instinct towards calmness in a crisis. It was rather reassuring to cling on to the kicking boat, and to be laid-back about it. I got no credit at all for this because, of course, everyone else assumed the new guy was too stupid to panic. Within a couple of minutes we were sorted out and back racing. I really began to feel like I'd never been away.

The Nab Tower was not very far away now, rusty, and with a noticeable lean. The leading boats were already rounding it and turning back for the homeward leg. I crouched on the side-deck, like a coiled spring, ready to discharge my function. My time was coming. My only job in the race was to help pull the spinnaker through the fore-hatch when it was taken down. Any minute now.

'Minute to the mark!' called the navigator, which was a bit superfluous, since the tower was looming over us.

'Ready for the drop?' called Dougal.

There was a scramble for positions. I scurried off the side-deck, and down the companionway. I heard the hatch being opened by the bowman. 'You there?' he called through it.

'Yep! Coming!' I scrambled forwards – there was an enormous quantity of sailing bags and kit on the cabin floor, thrown there during the broach. I got my foot tangled in the strap of a sailing bag, and fell over.

'OK!' called Dougal. 'Drop!'

I tried to scramble forward with the bag still attached, but the other strap was wedged behind the galley. I tried to take off my boot, but I'd tied a knot in a drawstring round the top, and despite an undisputed talent for knots (the only bit of sailing you can practise on your own in your bedroom) I couldn't get it undone. The boat rolled, and I fell over again. It was like Laurel and Hardy go yachting. Up forward, the spinnaker was being stuffed through the hatch from above, wet, yellow acres of it.

I finally got free and threw myself forward. I arrived just in time to land on top of the last of the spinnaker. 'Cheers!' said the bowman, and shut the hatch. I had made no contribution at all, and I hadn't even been missed.

I sat for a moment on the sail as the last drips of water from the hatch pattered on my oilskins. When I went back on deck, Beth said, 'Good job, well done.' They couldn't have done it without me.

The upwind sail back didn't have much to recommend it. It was cold. The wind and the by now pretty substantial waves it was kicking up meant that every few minutes green water would crash over us, with a shock of cold, and invariably a cold trickle down the back of your neck.

We were hiking the boat – getting our weight as far out on the windward side as possible to counterbalance the wind in the sails. I have no idea why it's called hiking. It may be because it's wet, cold and miserable and best performed in waterproof trousers. You sit in a row along the upwind edge of the deck, facing outwards, packed in shoulder-to-shoulder, your legs hanging over the side of the boat. Then you duck your head under the upper of the two horizontal lifelines, and drape yourself over the lower one so that it digs into your stomach and rearranges your internal organs. It's not comfortable, but it takes some weight off your buttocks and stops you losing the feeling in your legs. Waves hit you on the side of the head like a cold wet assault with a really big snowball.

The only relief is a tack, when you get to try to untangle yourself from the lifelines while those around you do the same. You all elbow each other in the head repeatedly, then cross the boat under the boom, and reassume your positions on the other side, on a cold wet deck. But for most of the time, for most of the crew, you just sit there. On an offshore race, you might sit there all night while everything from your brain outwards goes cold and numb, and your remaining sliver of consciousness amuses itself by hallucinating about sofas and central heating.

On one long, awful race in the Irish Sea when I was about seventeen, we did this for forty-eight hours straight, shivering like sheep in winter. All we had to eat were things called Hot Cans – a sort of chilli-con-carne-flavoured dog-food in a tin that heated itself up when you activated a ring-pull. There was little sympathy from the dryer, warmer guys at the back of the boat, and among those of us on the rail the talk of mutiny was perfectly serious. I finally fell asleep for a few minutes on the second night, and the two guys next to me started a conversation about whether, somewhere else in the galaxy, there were aliens doing just the same thing . . . and what they'd be saying to each other. When I woke up, the two of them were going, 'Beep! Beeeep! Reeepapapapa! Beep-beep!' I just assumed some bit of my brain had frozen and I'd lost the ability to understand language. It seemed a reasonable explanation, and I accepted it, and went back to sleep. I was disappointed when I didn't freeze to death completely.

Back to the finish was not that bad, and we tacked every few minutes, which helped us keep warm. But it still felt like a long trip. Into the Solent, past Ryde, and on along the island shore, a green filling in a sandwich of grey sea and grey sky. It was not a scintillating sail, but I was content. I was back on the weather rail, moving with the boat, being flecked with salt spray, feeling the occasional thump as we hit a wave.

It felt right, normal. Like going back to a town you once lived in, and finding that it's all more or less the same, even the things you'd forgotten about. After the first few minutes, it didn't even really feel like going back, and even then a lot of the strangeness was new people, new boat. It was all fine.

What was less clear was why doing this had once been an all-encompassing obsession. It had been nice to get back on a boat. It was good to feel the wind, watch the waves, and to be part of the magic that makes forward motion out of nothing more. I'd enjoyed it, and I'd be back again soon. But I hadn't felt anything truly profound. It was just something I could do, surprisingly well all things considered, but you could probably say the same about other teenage activities like A-level maths or playing Leonard Cohen's greatest hits on the tuba. Nothing had whispered to my soul.

I wasn't going to work it all out in one day. After all, apart from the broach it had been a dull race: not much excitement, and in the end, not much of a result. A turgid nil–nil on a grey afternoon probably wasn't where football obsessions took hold either, except in the minds of dull, unimaginative children with no internal life, and an inability to keep things in perspective.

I decided that, for the moment, it was probably best to ignore this thesis. It was costing Dougal a lot of money for me to be this cold and wet, and I owed it to him to enjoy it.

Finally we crossed the bay below Osborne House and rounded the point to the finish. It was clear that we hadn't covered ourselves in glory – we were in the kind of mid-fleet position that my younger self had learned to accept. No one on the boat really talked about it – though whether out of pent-up frustration or because they didn't really care, I had no idea. We crossed the finishing line to no fanfare whatever. Dougal called, 'OK, guys, thanks a lot, let's tidy up.' And that was that. It was a relief to get up and move about.

We headed back to the marina on the mainland side of the Solent. The sun finally came out. We tidied up the boat, folded the sails, and peeled off wet layers of clothing. Then we retired to a local pub, where we had a great deal to drink, and ate some truly awful food. We talked about the race — apparently we'd come within inches of hitting the tower, which I'd missed because I was down below doing slapstick sailing. No one ever mentioned a result.

I was happy enough. I'd managed the difficult bit – I was a sailor again. I was having a few beers with the crew, and doing what sailors always do: recalling events long past, and exaggerating them to the point of parody. When I headed off to the station to get a train home, Beth said she'd call the next week. Of course, she never did.

Chapter Five

Blaze of Glory

GROWING UP IN 1980S NORTHERN IRELAND WAS, FOR the most part, surprisingly normal. There were just a few oddities resulting from the political situation. For instance, I went to a school in an area of Belfast the very mention of which used to make my grandmother shudder. In particular, she always warned me about a bar up the road from the school, as if it was likely I might want to pop in for a swift half at lunchtime. Something had 'happened' there, though she would never tell me what.

The bar certainly was a threatening-looking place, with a huge wire fence in front of it to stop it from being petrol-bombed. But a lot of Belfast looked like that. And anyway, if you'd wanted to petrol-bomb it, the door was always standing open and welcoming, and you could have chucked your bomb straight in. Somehow that made it a lot less intimidating. Standing at the bus stop opposite waiting to go home, we used to spend hours debating how best to make a petrol-bomb.

There were even some aspects to growing up in the

Troubles that were rather nice. When you went on holiday outside Ireland, you always had a pleasing novelty value, among the English in particular. It was wearing for my parents because people made odd assumptions, and asked them lots of sometimes rather clumsy questions, but other children regarded me as having a bit of street-fighter cool.

I did as little as I could to disabuse them of this fancy. I told stories about the army patrols that used to walk past us while we waited for the bus home. (True.) The patrols, I explained, always came in fours, with a radio operator third in line, and a squaddie walking backwards at the rear. (True.) I told them about the time that Stephen Connor tripped up the guy walking backwards, and got shot. (Not true – squaddies who wanted to make it to their nineteenth birthday were not likely to be fooled by a thirteen-year-old sticking out a foot like Dennis the Menace.)

And I always, always, always let myself down by mentioning sailing. I'd just have successfully painted myself as a cross between Rambo and James Bond when I'd slip up. The spell would break, and my rapt audience's fantasy view of me would stop dead in its tracks. Triangulating with the aid of the class system, they would relocate me to an entirely different category, and start talking about something more interesting, invariably the English football team. Northern Ireland, and me with it, would lope back to the periphery of the British Isles, and I'd spend the rest of my holidays reading a book on my own.

Then one day, in Portugal, I met a kid from the Isle of Wight, and the roles were reversed. He was cool. He went to school in Cowes! Going to school in a war zone, especially one that only existed in the mind of my grandmother, had absolutely nothing on going to school in the Spiritual Home of Yachting™. Cowes was continually referred to in magazines and books, always with the casual assumption that anyone who had any right to read about sailing would be intimate with the place. There were never any descriptions, never any photos. This kid had been there. He must have seen all sorts of famous sailors, seen all the best boats.

Sadly, the only thing he hated more than sailing was the Isle of Wight and everything on it. He reserved a particular dislike for Cowes, and the Solent, which lay between him and his beloved Southampton FC. I learned nothing from him, apart from some stuff about Gary Lineker being a girl that I sat through in the hope that he might accidentally drop clues about his home into the conversation. He didn't.

This was terribly frustrating. You can imagine how wonderfully mysterious Cowes appeared to someone who did their yachting at Carrickfergus. Well, you probably can't. Anyone with any sense at all can guess what Cowes is like – there is a limit to how exotic a small town on an island off southern England can be. But for me Cowes was everything that I wanted but did not have.

The Solent would not involve much sewage, or jellyfish dodging. The clear blue water would glitter in the sunlight. Schools of dolphins would play around your boat, and perhaps offer tactical advice. There was every probability that in the clubhouse bar afterwards a star like Harold Cudmore would be on hand to tell me what I was doing wrong, and that he'd recognise my latent talent and appoint himself to be my personal coach. In Cowes I'd be a much better sailor. In Cowes I would win. I really believed this – and bear in mind I was taking a thumping at every race from all sorts of kids who were quite obviously never going to amount to very much.

It's as well I never saw the place when I was fourteen. Nowhere on earth could have measured up to my expectations. But, as it turned out, especially not Cowes.

Cowes is a small town, with steep hills and narrow streets. The sea and the river Medina aren't even terribly apparent from most of the high street. It looks and feels like any number of small towns from Norfolk to Northumberland, except for the unexpectedly high incidence of cheap Italian restaurants, and several shops devoted to the sale of photographs of boats. Look closer, and you realise that quite a few of the 'hardware' shops are chandlers. My favourite was a shop with a window display of nautical oddments, and a dog's life jacket – which surprised me, since I had a notion that dogs floated.

Cowes still feels more worldly than its equivalent in Norfolk or Northumberland, although it's not immediately clear why. It's the capital of the Isle of Wight, though I'm not sure how much cosmopolitan flash that's worth. It might have something to do with its position in the world of yachting, like St Andrews and golf. But I suspect that matters only to a particular type of traditionalist.

I think the answer is best illustrated by going down to the Town Quay and catching a water taxi up river, past the chain ferry. A Cowes water taxi bears little resemblance to its Venetian cousin – there's not much varnish or polished brass, but plenty of chipped fibreglass and plywood, and an inch of brackish water swilling around the bottom. Any singing your driver does is likely to lack finesse. It's more of a water mini-cab. But at least they're fairly cheap. And from the river, Cowes looks different.

It has the anatomy of a shipbuilding town, which is what Cowes was for most of the last five hundred years. Big industrial sheds line the banks, behind and between the marinas. There are cranes and chimneys, and slipways lead to the water. It doesn't match the neat, permed high street. Like Belfast, Glasgow and other shipbuilding towns, it's always looked out at the world. It's even looked beyond that – the Black Arrow, the only UK rocket ever to launch a satellite, was built in Cowes in 1971.

Of course, in the 1980s I didn't know about any of this, and wouldn't have cared if I had. Cowes was yachting, Cowes Week, the Fastnet Race, the Royal Yacht Squadron. It was where the America's Cup got its name, when a challenge match in 1851 was won by the schooner *America*. These and a hundred other jumbled-up events and places rattled round my head, with no context or even an accompanying mental slide-show.

I was sure that Cowes was going to be a significant place in my life, because it was where all the famous sailors lived. I was never anything other than a conformist, so it was clearly where I would live too. It made sense – the locals would be used to seeing sailing stars around the place, so autograph-hunters wouldn't continually bother me, as they would anywhere else.

This was an important consideration. After the Australians won the America's Cup in 1983, I, and everyone else, thought sailing was on the edge of going mainstream. It feels like a silly thing to even say now. But I approached it with all the perspective of a twelve-year-old, and anyway, I wasn't the only one taken in. Channel 4 were right there with me when they paid for the television rights for the next edition, four years later in 1987. The sport looked hi-tech, glitzy, and the two-boat match-race format meant it was almost, but not quite, comprehensible on television.

To illustrate, a bit over-literally, how fashionable sailing had become, Patrick Lichfield turned up with several tanned models in thin white swimsuits, whom he posed artfully on boats, cranes and docks, while apparently conducting a continual TV interview over his shoulder. It says much for my naivety that I was the only heterosexual adolescent boy in history to be annoyed by semi-naked women obscuring the view.

There were daily updates in the papers. The key players were, if not quite household names, certainly well-known to general sports fans, and there was perfectly straight-faced coverage of an attempt to sell a stolen copy of the designs for the British entry's keel to the New York Yacht Club.

Of course, it all went wrong. We probably deserved it. I certainly deserved it. The first disaster was that my heroes in the British team were distinctly under-whelming. The second was that the *Australia 2* team failed to recreate their crushing form of 1983. And it wasn't just me; these were also the two outfits that had received most of the UK media's attention. Their failure meant that long before the final races, interest had started to dribble away.

Meanwhile, Dennis Conner, the American skipper

beaten in 1983, had quietly formed his own team. While everyone else moved to the regatta's base in Western Australia, he trained in Hawaii, where no one could easily spy on him. He arrived late at the event, largely written off by me and by all the other experts, sand-bagged his way through the qualifying rounds, reached the final against a gang of Australians none of us had heard of, stopped faking, and whitewashed them 4–0 in the best-of-seven series without apparently breaking sweat. The premium corporate-hospitality packages weren't even scheduled to start until race five. And that was disaster number three. (Although it's possible that's not how Dennis Conner saw it.)

It looked like things couldn't get any worse, so naturally they did. Just as everyone was preparing to move to Conner's home port of San Diego for a 1989 or 1990 cup, disaster four arrived. The Kiwis suddenly challenged under the original rules of the Cup's Deed of Gift, rules that had been sidelined by convention for years. They wanted a one-on-one showdown, and they wanted it at very short notice in a new class of yacht. By happy coincidence, the only existing yacht of the class was owned by a Kiwi businessman.

It is, in general, unwise to argue the smallprint of anything with a group of well-funded Americans. They responded with months of litigation, on the basis that they were not going to let themselves be bested at their national sport of looking for loopholes. The Cup might still have had a chance to settle as a global sporting fixture, but instead it got bogged down in the courts for years.

By this point I didn't know or care what was going on, and if I, of all people, didn't care it seems a good bet that no one else cared either. The America's Cup dropped out of the sports pages, taking most of the sport's public profile with it.[10]

The America's Cup finally came back to Cowes when the town hosted a 150th Anniversary regatta in 2001. It was an exhibition event, for which *Australia 2* was taken out of mothballs in a Sydney museum and shipped over, complete with her '83 crew. If I'd known, I'd have gone to see that, sailor or not. I saw *Australia 2* in her museum in 1999, and it was an embarrassingly emotional experience. I once mocked in print the kind of moist-eyed cycling fan who idolised the bike Eddy Merckx used to break the world hour record. I'd obviously forgotten that my personal history contained an episode where I had burst into tears and tried to hug a keel.

It was early in the morning on Good Friday, and I was taking a taxi up the river in Cowes to *Blaze of Glory*, the boat I'd signed up for at the RORC party. I was sorry that Beth from *Afterglow* hadn't made contact again – I'd enjoyed the sail with them. But, on the other hand, Mike and Helen had seemed nice enough at the party. *BoG* was bigger, newer and considerably shinier than *Afterglow*. While the latter was a well-used ten-year-old boat, *BoG* was so new that when I'd come down the previous

---

[10] The Cup did get going again a few years later, as an almost entirely new event with heavy commercial sponsorship displacing the old Corinthian amateurism, and logos all over the boats and sails. But the moment had passed; the only time it showed up on the TV news was when *oneAustralia* broke in half, and sank within seconds off San Diego in 1995. Just for the record, the last logo to vanish beneath the waves was that of Foster's lager, who were no doubt delighted with this demonstration of how easily their product went down.

weekend, the rest of the crew were removing plastic packaging. This was her very first regatta, a three-day event over the Easter Weekend.

The boat, all £250,000 of it, was owned by Mac, who I hadn't met, but of whose fabulousness I had heard much. Helen's slightly sheepdog-like 'He's a wonderful owner' at the RORC party was echoed by the rest of the crew. It was slightly, very slightly, like a cult.

At 45 feet she was 5 feet longer than *Afterglow*. Down below, there were vast amounts of shiny wood, and a saloon table you could have played table tennis on. The navigator at the adjacent chart table could have kept score, which, much to his frustration, was about all the many thousands of pounds' worth of electronics and computer systems seemed to be up to.

The GPS system, for instance, maintained – in the face of any amount of evidence to the contrary – that the boat was somewhere in the foothills of Mont Blanc. It resisted all assaults on this opinion by the navigator, IT support, and the firm that supplied the GPS, until some months later a member of the crew discovered that placing a pair of damp underpants over the antenna did the trick.

But that wasn't my problem. It was a step towards my blue-skies, blue-seas dream, and I was a fully paid-up member of the crew – the bowman. This is an important, responsible, skilled position, and hence just the job to entrust to a random bloke you picked out of the crowd at a party on the basis that he was about the right size.

I was very pleased to have managed, so quickly, not just to get a bit of sailing sorted out, but to actually get into a proper position on a proper crew. I'd imagined many weeks of hanging around as a floating, spare member of crew, proving myself, and working my way up. Somehow I'd managed, without really trying, to convince a credible-looking outfit that I was competent, trustworthy and a real asset. The logical sequence that started with my knowing I was probably not any of these things and finished with my having enough faith in these people's judgement to entrust my safety to them at sea clearly had a gap in it somewhere, but I decided to ignore it.

Bowmen like to imagine themselves as the lead guitar players of the crew. This has been the case ever since they changed the name of the job from 'deck-hand', which had a regrettable lack of glamour, and is perilously close to 'dick-head'. They credit themselves with unfeasibly large quotas of cool on the basis that they get wetter than anyone else on the boat, colder, and, occasionally, have to climb up masts or out spinnaker poles to fix problems.

The bowman runs the show at the front of the boat. He organises sail changes, and during a gybe he swaps the spinnaker pole from one corner of the sail to the other. At the start he helps the helmsman by standing at the point of the bow making hand signals to indicate how far it is to the start-line, and what other boats there are around. The signals are complicated, and every bowman seems to have a different system, but that doesn't matter, since most helmsmen ignore them anyway. They look cool, and that's the important bit.

Despite the best attempts of the bowman fraternity over the years to make this look like quantum physics, none of it is all that complicated. Not in theory anyway. What makes it difficult is that you have to do it all on a sloping deck that bounces up and down, and is often underwater altogether. The numerous bits of rope for which the bowman is responsible all look the same, and are horribly easy to get tangled up. When combined with a sail that has the area of a three-bedroom flat's floorplan, a tangle can produce chaos on a properly epic scale. Being a bowman is mainly about avoiding mistakes.

BoG's very first race was actually all right. With me standing on the bow wearing my best sunglasses and making enthusiastic if non-committal hand gestures, Mike got us to within a length of the line as the starting-gun went. He was a little tentative, but with a week-old boat, I could appreciate the urge not to scratch anything, especially since Mac wasn't with us for his boat's first race.

I moved back down the boat and took my place at the front of the crew sitting along the weather rail. 'That looked bloody competent,' said the guy next to me. 'You really know the hand signals, yeah?' It was as strange a compliment as it sounds, but it was nice to make a positive impression so soon.

It was very quiet on board. Normally that's a good sign, everyone concentrating, no idle chat. But even the necessary flow of information between the trimmers and the helmsman was missing. The boat felt dead – the crew on the rail looked absently around them waiting for something to happen when they should have been watching the fleet so they'd be ready for whatever was going to happen next.

Still, a new boat and all that, and maybe the only aim was to get round the first race or two and have a think about it afterwards. We sailed out close-hauled to the right-hand side of the course, and tacked for the mark. The navigator, who called the tack, was spot on, even without the magic underpants. I got the spinnaker bag on deck, dragged it forwards, and went to the leeward deck to connect it up. It was a breezy day, and I got a comprehensive soaking down there. It's a vulnerable place to be, right on the leeward rail – there is an awful lot of water flying about the place, and it's difficult for anyone else on the crew to watch you in case you get washed clear off the boat. I got a couple of big cold April waves over me that made my head sing, and I seemed to spend forever fumbling about trying simply to connect three ropes to the three corners of a sail.

At the mark, the spinnaker popped up, and filled with wind, all rather neatly. I and the mast-man – the other member of the bow team – pulled down the jib, and fastened it down. This is all quite physical, the sails are big and surprisingly heavy, and the composite sailcloth is stiff and slippery, and difficult to work with. I was simultaneously pleased and disappointed when several of the crew were visibly impressed at the speed with which I did all this – pleased because, well, any kind of ego rub is worth having; disappointed because it suggested the standards on the boat were not set awfully high.

We finished well down the fleet, but we hadn't had any major disasters. Our big problem seemed, to me anyway, to be that the boat didn't go fast enough for enough of the time. There were occasional flashes that, if we could reproduce reliably, would put us well up the order, but there didn't appear to be any system in place for keeping track of the settings.

I tried to start a conversation about it, but it was clear that this was not regarded as my job. *BoG* was not a democratic boat.

There were two more races that day. I remembered

that at the RORC party skipper Mike had mentioned that they considered themselves an offshore crew, attuned to the more relaxed rhythms of long races over several days rather than the short blitzes of inshore racing, and several of the crew looked knackered.

We were spending the weekend sleeping on the boat, in the marina. I hate sleeping on boats. Normally everyone tries very hard to find somewhere to stay on land, because whatever the brochure might have to say about a forest's-worth of teak, lavishly appointed galley, en-suite heads, and exquisite Italian craftsmanship, when you sleep on a boat it turns into a caravan. A caravan with pointy ends, a very low ceiling, few windows and little ventilation. Take it from me, the only thing that affects your comfort is how many of you have to sleep on it at once.

A boat with six berths will sleep about four people at an only mildly intolerable level of discomfort. A boat with eight berths will sleep about four, and a boat with ten berths will sleep about four. Any boat with more berths than that will never sleep anyone at all, since an owner who can afford a boat that size can also afford a few hotel rooms, or, indeed, a few hotels.

Blaze of Glory had nine berths. There were nine of us on her. We still managed eight hours of good-quality sleep. Unfortunately, that averaged out at less than an hour each.

Space wasn't the only issue. I was sharing a double berth with Bill, the mast-man, an Accident and Emergency consultant who snored like he was trying to get through to a humpback whale somewhere off the Falklands. The whole boat resonated. It was like trying to sleep inside a double bass. After a few hours, I got up and went on deck.

In the quiet orange light I could see concentric rings of ripples radiating from the boat. They carried Bill's acoustic signature out into the ocean. They were quite pretty actually, and it was interesting to see how they echoed the vibrations of the deck. I watched them for a while, then went and slept on the dock. It rained, but I didn't mind. Anything is better than sleeping on a boat.

The following day was much like the previous, with the exception that the famous Mac finally turned up. We hadn't been sure he'd make it at all – he'd been away on a business trip (£250,000 boats don't buy themselves, you know) and he'd only just got back. He rang from the ferry. The mood on the boat was ecstatic: 'Mac's here!' 'How wonderful.' 'We'll really get some sailing done now Mac's here.' 'Mac's coming? Brilliant.' A complete stranger walking down the marina overheard, and said, 'Mac's coming? That's great!' He wasn't being sarcastic. Mac's fame clearly spread far beyond BoG.

Contrary to my expectations, Mac didn't arrive accompanied by a piper. He was a fit-looking man of late middle age, handsome and rather charismatic. He said hello, and flashed a broad, conspiratorial grin at me. I don't think he even noticed that, since I'd been getting changed when he arrived, I hadn't been wearing trousers. If he had, he clearly didn't mind. All the same, I was immediately taken aside by another of the crew and soundly ticked off for a breach of decorum. I was never to appear before Mac inappropriately attired. It was a ticking-off that wouldn't have seemed out of place in the Long Room at Lord's but it felt a bit peculiar on a racing-yacht at breakfast time. I was beginning to wonder just how I was going to fit in here for a season.

A suspicion that the crew of *BoG* were, to use the technical term, as odd as fuck was beginning to occur to me.

I ought, in fairness, to point out that owners come in many guises, and have just as many different relationships with their crew. Some, like Dougal from *Afterglow*, are owner–skippers, who own the show and run the show. Others let someone else take responsibility for the boat and sail as a member of the crew, albeit one you don't want to accidentally whack with a winch-handle. Some want to be one-of-the-guys; some, particularly the older ones, rather pointedly don't. I'd met owners who were blokes, chaps, wide-boys, wankers, rock stars, racists, syndicates and Nazis. I'd never met one who insisted on being a deity.

Mac didn't seem, so far as I could see, to insist on it either. But the respect with which he was held was quite something. I was impressed, though admittedly not to the point of worship, by discovering that he'd been the bowman on a famous offshore racer of the 1970s, part of an Admiral's Cup-winning team captained by Ted Heath. He was surprised I'd even heard of it.

Mac let Mike skipper the boat, but he liked to take the helm personally. Cue 'Whoooo! Go, Mac! You show 'em!' type cheers. We did actually bump, rather gently, with another boat on the starting-line of the second day's first race. Everyone was too polite to mention it. We hit the same boat again at the fourth mark. They were surprised to see us again, and they were very clear on the point – we were to stop crashing into them immediately if we could possibly help it. On most boats there would have been some (probably) good-natured piss-taking. On

BoG there was only silence while everyone checked their boots for scuffs.

Our results on day two were in line with the results from day one. We lost Mac for most of the second and third races to a prolonged conference call down below. ('It's a shame Mac's not here,' I said. Everyone looked baffled. Clearly I hadn't got the hang of this.) I managed to avoid any terrible mistakes, and the one sizeable error I made I remedied by climbing to the end of the spinnaker pole, high above the water. Most of the crew were so impressed with this that they forgot that the only reason for the acrobatics was that I'd screwed up to begin with.

We finished the regatta somewhere in the middle of the fleet. That's a euphemism. What sailors do is stop caring after a certain point – the placings go first, second, third, fourth, fifth, and everything else is 'the middle of the fleet'. I don't really know where we ended up. The boat showed some occasional speed, so I doubt that we were awful. But we could have done better.

And that was the feeling I had too. I'd kicked off the weekend genuinely delighted to have sorted out some sailing, and to be a proper part of the team. But I took the train home on Sunday evening exhausted from the exertion and the lack of sleep, and with some real doubts about the team I'd signed up for. They were nice enough, and they were reasonable company for a quiet night in the pub near where the boat was moored. But from the gents' loo in the pub, you could hear the music echoing across the water from the parties going on in the town centre. I'm not the kind of person who would walk across broken glass to get to a disco (although when I got there

I would dance as if I had). I probably wouldn't even walk across the road. But there was a deathly chime of impending middle-age about sitting in a pub listening to a good time drifting across the river on the night air, while drinking bitter, eating chicken in a basket and discussing whether the best route from London to Southampton was via the M3 or the A3.

On the water, *BoG* was sailed very competently. Mike was a meticulous skipper, and on an offshore race I'd have very happily entrusted my life to him. There hadn't been much sign of an aggressive edge to our racing, but Mike had always said that the boat's aim for the season was the 450-mile race to La Rochelle in August, which would take several days. The problem is that the guys who win offshore events also win inshore events like the one we'd just done. It's like bike racing – someone who can beat you over 10 miles will probably beat you over 100. The pace changes, but the skill and ability required remain the same.

The other, selfish element to my concern was that I'd turned out to be more competent than I'd expected. The opposite would hardly have been possible. Initially I'd wanted nothing more than someone, anyone, to take me on. Now that I'd found that, I wanted more. Enough is never enough. I hadn't gone to the Commonwealth Games for a holiday – I wanted to be competitive. I couldn't help it. The *BoG* experience had just felt a bit woolly.

I didn't plan to abandon them altogether – there were several events in the year they were doing that I wanted to do, like Cowes Week and the La Rochelle race. But if I got a better offer, I knew I'd take it.

This was ungrateful. But if there was one thing I remembered from last time round, it was that if anyone was going to enjoy their sailing, it was essential that a crew work harmoniously. Different boats have different atmospheres – largely based on the owner and skipper's personalities (measured on the bloke-to-Nazi scale), the age of the crew, and what they want from their hobby. One of the things about *BoG* that had made me uncomfortable was the earnestness of it – there was very little of the wise-cracking that I expected, and a couple of slightly sarcastic remarks I'd made had clearly been taken rather too much to heart. Boats can be awfully small places. They hadn't worked it out yet, but they wanted rid of me too.

Stephen Dobbs was a prominent figure in my life for several years because I couldn't race a Mirror on my own. We'd started sailing together at one of the Carrickfergus sailing schools, where helms and crews were assigned almost randomly. I initially took a liking to him because he knew more dirty jokes than anyone else I'd ever met.

It was immediately clear from his command of the vernacular that Dobbs was an exceptional personality. He claimed to have bedded most of the girls in school, even those who were obviously physically repelled by him, as well as the daughter of the bloke who ran the sailing school, a girl who could kill a teenage boy with a single scornful glance. Most of his acquaintances were taken in by this for rather longer than we really cared to admit.

There were other incidents, like the occasion I entered us in the Scout sailing championships, and told him to keep quiet about the fact he wasn't in the Scouts and never had been, only for him to turn up in a ludicrous Baden-Powell outfit that he'd found in a trunk in his parents' loft, complete with knee socks and hat. We might still have got off with it if he hadn't told some Guides an obscene joke about woggles.

It was a shame, since there was no single event on the calendar where there was a lower standard of sailing – I think I'd come third the previous year with a different crew, who was in the Scouts, but who couldn't sail and who just sat in the boat grinning vacantly while I did all the work. (In many respects he was an ideal crew, but his family emigrated to Australia a few weeks afterwards.) Sailing was deadly serious, and I grew to hate the degree of sarcastic levity with which Dobbs approached it. But crew were hard to find – Mirrors were not awfully expensive, and lots of kids had their own boat but no crew. Dobbs was available and competent, which meant I was stuck with him.

The bigger tensions arose directly from my cack-handed waggling of the tiller. Normally we'd manage to get the boat rigged, down the slipway and into the water without hostilities breaking out. Then I'd make an atrocious start – quite an achievement in a Mirror, since they go so slowly – and he'd start a sort of work-to-rule, sitting grumpily in the front of the cockpit, obeying orders to the letter with a contemptuous degree of precision, and not doing anything more. If I ever laid hands upon a rope that was on his side of the demarcation, he would refuse to touch it again that race.

He was prepared to take this to ridiculous lengths. On one windy race, I freed a jib sheet (his side of the demarcation) that had snagged during a tack. He refused to touch it again. We capsized a few moments later. This was unusual in a Mirror; they have small sails and are very hard to knock over. It's not impossible that there may have been some incompetence involved.

A capsized dinghy will float on its side – the mast prevents complete inversion. To right it, I had to swim round to the underside and climb onto the centreboard. Mirrors float very high, so to get onto the board, I needed a rope tossed over the high side of the boat to help me climb. Guess which rope.

'Your jib sheet, you come and get it.'

'Please, Dobbs. I'm freezing.'

'Nah. I like it better this way up. I think it'll go faster. Anyway, I thought this was what you wanted? Otherwise you'd have eased the mainsheet when the gust hit. That's what people do when they don't want to capsize.'

Underlying all this was the suspicion on my part that Dobbs might actually be better at sailing than me. I was in charge because I was the owner, and I wanted to be in charge, and because Dobbs was very well suited to his role as an insubordinate little shit. He wouldn't have been able to cope with the pressures of command.

Or so I thought. One Tuesday evening we had a furious row – not the usual sulky silence, a proper row. We'd actually been doing quite well, for once, and as usual when that happened, a sort of truce had broken out. Then we had a bad leg, and lost enough ground to put us near the back again. What was really unfair about that was that it wasn't really my fault – the wind had shifted quite dramatically, and left us and another boat, not incidentally the boat that won most of the Carrickfergus Mirror events, out on the wrong side of the course.

Dobbs flipped. He ranted and swore at me, how he should have found a proper helmsman, not a talentless wanker like me. I, fatefully, replied in the following ill-advised terms: 'So I suppose you think you could do better?'

'Fucking right I could,' he said.

This is not the correct form of words for a mutiny. What he should have said was, 'Will you retire to your cabin, sir?' But I could see that he meant business.

We swapped places. Even with me crewing in the spirit in which Dobbs usually did the job, we started to peg our way back. We picked up a lucky shift on the next leg, and one of the boats in front managed to drop their little Mirror-sized spinnaker in the water and then sail over it and stop dead. I couldn't see what Dobbs was doing that was different to me, but things just seemed to work out for him. I was too craven to demand we abandon the race and retire while I still had some dignity left. By the finish he'd clawed us up to second place – our best result of that season. It was at least partly luck, but that didn't make any difference. Even I was smart enough not to try to argue about it.

In fact, neither of us said anything at all. We took the boat ashore, de-rigged it in silence and put the dinghy-cover on. We both knew what had happened. We never sailed together again.

33208 herself was never quite the same for me after that. I had loved her, really, deeply, as I've adored no other 'inanimate' object. I'd spent some of the happiest hours of my life in the garage with her, sanding, varnishing, going over her inch by inch, cleaning and polishing her until she shone. And now I felt I'd let her down.

I sailed her for the rest of that season, and part of the next. I even spent a preposterous amount of money on buying her a new spinnaker – I remember it being over £100, and it was certainly the most expensive thing I'd ever bought. I think I bought it to say sorry to her.

With it, she was a boat transformed. Whereas before I'd lost 20 yards on every downwind leg, now I was passing other boats without even trying, and could gain enough ground that my iffy upwind speed was not a disaster. Sailing with a different crew, I almost won the following series, losing out only to a guy who subsequently won the Irish Championships.

But, as I said, the love was gone. And anyway, it was too late. Mirrors are for kids. By the time I was finally winning, I was already about 70kg, which almost sank the back of the boat. (Indeed the best hypothesis for Dobbs's success was that since he was lighter than me, by changing places, we finally got the fore-and-aft trim of the boat right. But I know I'm scrabbling, and after twenty years it's a bit undignified.)

33208 was sold. I only realised when I started digging through my parents' loft in preparation for writing this book that I don't even have a photograph of her.

Chapter Six

Moorish Idol

I DON'T REMEMBER IT HAPPENING, AND I STILL CAN'T quite believe it did, but sometime in early 1982 my father must have started a conversation with my mother with a sentence along the lines of: 'I've had a great idea, why don't we go for a cruise up the west coast of Scotland for the family holiday this year?'

I can only assume that when Mum said yes to this patently lunatic suggestion, she thought she was calling his bluff. My mother's dislike of sailing was legendary. Most of our family holidays consisted of sitting for a fortnight in a cottage in the west of Ireland listening to rain beating against the window and bickering about who was going to go out into the storm and cycle five miles to the shop to buy more gin. It wasn't perfect, but at least no one got seasick, and I got lots of exercise. A cruising holiday felt more like a dare than a rational scheme for family relaxation.

We invited another family, so that there would be another competent sailor in the party and so that Tim (a couple of years older than me) and Sarah (a year younger) would be permanently on hand to make fun of me for having glasses and a terrible squint – 'Hey, four-eyes, can you see round corners?' I took with me a copy of *A Night to Remember*, Walter Lord's book about the sinking of the *Titanic*, which I read while holding the book up in front of my face so that everyone could read the title. At the time I reckoned it was just about the funniest thing anyone had ever done.

The cruise was not a stunning success. Given the puppyish enthusiasm with which I approached a whole week afloat, and excitements like sailing in the dark, sleeping on a boat (it's more fun when you're a kid) and rowing ashore for milk before breakfast like in *Swallows and Amazons*, my noticing that it wasn't quite perfect suggests it must have been awful.

We started out with an overnight sail from Carrickfergus to Campbelltown, on the tip of the Mull of Kintyre. My diary suggests this was more exciting than Christmas Eve:

A brilliant night! Stayed up till 3.30, but I wasn't tired. Dad let me take bearings on all the lighthouses, and work out their flashing patterns so I could find them on the chart, then draw the lines on it to see where we were. It was really easy. Dad checked I'd got it right, but he didn't need to. It was just great. Mum spent the night being sick in a bucket.

Then, after a night tied up alongside a foul-smelling fishing-boat in Campbelltown, we sailed through Kilbrannan Sound and up Loch Fyne to Tarbert. In the sound we came across a basking shark (*'Shaaark!'*), which Dad poked with a boat-hook to see if anything interesting happened. I was terrified.

We got stormbound in Tarbert. I sent postcards to everyone I knew just so I could use the word 'stormbound'. We were stuck for three days. I remember wet streets, hours spent watching an ancient, weather-beaten fisherman gutting fish on the quay at a speed that was mesmerising, and getting soaked exploring the harbour in a rubber dinghy in the pouring rain with Tim and Sarah.

I caught my first ever fish in Tarbert, off an old wooden jetty near the harbour mouth. It was a pollack, which was a great deal bigger in my memory than it is in the picture I found of me holding it triumphantly by the tail. I killed it so that I could take it back to the boat. I must have looked as if I was beating a goldfish to death with a brick. Mum was delighted when I demanded it be cooked for tea.

Eventually we left Tarbert in a flat calm and more pouring rain, and went through the Kyles of Bute, a series of island sounds known for their beauty, but which we could barely see through the rain. We stopped at Inverkip near Glasgow, then went on to Troon. In Troon, Sarah insisted we go to a swimming pool, which just seemed wrong. We ought to have manfully jumped off the boat as she sailed along, and hauled ourselves back aboard with a rope streamed over the stern. Going to play on an inflatable octopus seemed undignified, so I sulked, and got a smack. I was sure that kind of thing never happened to Francis Chichester. Finally we sailed to Portpatrick, then home.

Mum had set the pattern for her holiday on the first

night. She was alternately seasick and appalled at the living conditions. It was like seven people living in a large holdall. I'm hard pressed to believe Dad had much fun either. He wasn't really a cruising sailor at heart; he liked his sailing to be competitive, and above all manly. A wet July trailing round Scotland in a cramped 30-footer with three excited children in tow must have failed to press any of the basic buttons for a good time. It was an experiment that was not repeated, and indeed I don't think the cruise has ever been mentioned in the family since.

Dad was a dutiful, if not obviously enthusiastic parent. He always found time to come to school plays and concerts, if only because he needed a laugh. On the way home from a primary school open day he accused the string orchestra for which I played second violin of being the worst thing he'd ever heard. This was a fair point – the orchestra consisted of a group of eight-year-olds who'd been given an instrument each and left to teach themselves. Our only help was a spotty graduate teacher who told us when to start and stop, and explained to the audience that the noise that had happened in between was called 'To The Garden Annie Went'. I still think it was mean of Dad to be quite that honest. But at least he came.

It was, however, obvious that Dad's idea of a really good time didn't feature me tagging along. The highlight of his year was, ironically, a trip with his racing crew to Tarbert at the end of May for the five-day Scottish Series. He started going shortly after I was born, and through my childhood I spent the last week of May in a tightly wound ball of frustration because I wasn't allowed to come along. I could tell by the zonked expression on Dad's face when he got home that it must have been indescribably wonderful. That didn't stop me trying to make him describe it.

His vague recollections simply added fuel to the fire, as did his very occasional phone calls home, always infectiously cheerful, and with loud music blaring in the background. The traditional structure of Christian values that my school tried to inculcate was undermined by my certain knowledge that heaven was Tarbert. I could find it on a map, just at the kink in the Mull of Kintyre.

As I reached my teens, it began to occur to me that the consumption of great quantities of alcohol might explain much of what made Tarbert so wonderful. This did not in any way diminish its appeal. The problem was that even when I got to an age where Dad could have taken me to Tarbert without having to explain himself to the Social Services afterwards, I had exams.

While my talent for doing exams was not in dispute, the consensus seemed to be that it was enhanced rather than diminished by my not being allowed to spend the week before they started drinking five times my body weight in Tennent's 80/- and chasing whatever limited bits of skirt were available. Most teenage dreams revolve around drinking and sex. This was drinking and sex and sailing.

I finally went to the Scottish Series during a four-day break in my first-year college exams. It was even more wonderful than I had hoped; four days that shine in my memory as if they were from a different, better life. The colourful little town, so much brighter than its grey Northern Irish equivalent, the larger-than-life people, the picturesque displays of public intoxication, and the convivial atmosphere of a stag-night that had gone feral and returned to the wild.

I didn't actually do any sailing at all. I, bizarrely, revised for my exams in a hungover stupor in the bar of the Tarbert Hotel during the day, and then drank all night. I returned to my college friends with a zonked expression on my face, and a somewhat vague idea of what I'd been doing for the last four days. It turned out that I couldn't remember any of the revision either, which was a shame, because, firstly, I could have gone sailing after all, and, secondly, I failed an exam that my tutor had assured me only a 'cretin' could fail, an opinion she reiterated even as she signed the bit of paper that ejected me from the department.[11]

The thought of going back to Tarbert had been a considerable attraction when I made the plans for my comeback. The chance to go back to those warm, long summer evenings and to actually go sailing on the fantastically lovely Loch Fyne would have justified the year on its own. Add to that the promise of the world's greatest party, and the lure was irresistible.

I was confident it would be the highlight of the season, if only I could find a boat. But I couldn't. Few English boats make the long trip, and despite phoning the only couple of people I even remotely knew in Northern Ireland who might be going, I drew a blank. The only offer I had was from a charter outfit, who wanted me to pay over £1,000 for a (discounted!) package, and I didn't much fancy that. Paying for me to have fun was what people like Mac were for. Much to my frustration, it

---

[11] At least I didn't take the route of a friend who declared that if you were going to revise drunk, you'd obviously better do the exam drunk too. He crashed through his exams like a teenage joyrider through a police road-block, and was never seen again.

looked like another Tarbert was going to slip by without me.

'UP! UP, you fuckwits! Get UP!'

I'm standing right on the bow of a 48-footer, trying to get the boat alongside to make some room for us on the start-line. I back up the suggestion with some polite hand signals. 'UP!'

The black boat gets out of the way – if they'd had any sense at all they'd have stayed where they were. I wasn't asking them to move for their benefit. I hold up three fingers – we're three lengths from the line – and give a thumbs-up to tell the helmsman that he has space to leeward to bear off if he likes.

The water is a cold-looking blue, with a few white-caps, and the breeze is strong. And all around is the simply beautiful, fjord-like coastline of Loch Fyne, with deep-pile forests and sheer rock-faces. This is it. I made it after all. The day before the regatta started the skipper of one of the biggest boats at the event had sent me an email – he needed a bowman, and he'd found my name on a 'crew seeking boat' web-page. Half an hour later one of Dad's old friends rang to say I could have the room he'd had on a rolling booking for twenty years in the Tarbert Hotel since he couldn't make it this year. This was heaven on a standby ticket. I dropped everything and headed north. I grinned like an idiot for all of the eight-hour drive from London.

In the last few seconds before the gun goes, the boats are tightly packed, pitching on the choppy water. Start-lines have collisions, and lots of shouting, lots of aggression. The shorter the line, the harder everyone has to fight to make space. We've done well: we have space to weather, obligingly vacated by the black boat, which means that in a few seconds when the race starts we'll have our own clean wind, not stuff that's been slowed down by blowing over another boat's sails. I give a thumbs-down to the helm: we can't bear off any more, we need to come up a bit.

The helmsman is fantastic. He's as good as I once thought I was going to be. I look at my watch: fifteen seconds to the start. The line is about one and a half boat-lengths away, and we're in the front row of boats. I'd say this was going to be about perfect.

'Trim on!' I shout – time to trim the sails in, get some speed. Not really my job to shout things like that, but standing at the front you begin to feel like a conductor. In reality, you're more like the bloke with the table tennis bats on the apron of an airport. You can wave your arms till they hurt, but however cool you think you look, you ain't actually driving.

The sails are trimmed and the boat starts to pick up some speed. I can see the full length of the line, from the race officer's boat to the buoy at the port end. We're about 3 feet in front of anyone else, the line is a length away (one finger), half a length (a fist) and bang! That was damn nearly perfect. On the line at the gun, with the boat moving well. I run aft down the deck, crouching to keep my balance, and take my place on the weather deck. The black boat I yelled at could have been right beside us with a bit more balls – but now they're three lengths behind. We are in the lead. It has been a few minutes of superb sailing.

Our boat was called *Moorish Idol* (named after a kind of dentist's waiting-room fish). Her helmsman, bizarrely, was a famous racing sailor called Gery Trentesaux. Before the summer was out, he would captain a French team to victory in the Commodore's Cup. I had absolutely no idea what the hell he was doing on a boat that twenty-four hours previously was scraping around for crew from iffy websites. Maybe he'd been kidnapped and brain-washed. It seemed the most rational explanation.

That doesn't mean I wasn't glorying in sitting at the front of the rail on this big, sexy boat, being driven by a sailor who got his picture in magazines. This was, I felt, more like it. In subsequent conversations I may have inadvertently given the impression that Gery had hand-picked me for his team, but I really don't think anyone can blame me for that. This was the kind of thing I'd dreamed about.

We just flew up the first leg. Gery steered with a precise confidence, his mate Glen trimmed the headsail and made tactical calls. I arranged my features into a pose of serious yet handsome concentration for a passing photographer's boat. It's hard to be certain – boats carry time handicaps that are tricky to work out mid-race – but I reckon that at the first mark we were in the lead. I began to speculate on the possibility of being, by sheer luck, on a Tarbert-winning crew.

Dad came here for year after year, and never won. I could just imagine sending him a smug text announcing that at the first time of asking I'd managed what he hadn't. And maybe following it up with some smug phone calls and maybe some magazine clippings. I'd enjoy that.

The problem was that the rest of us weren't up to Gery's standard. At the first mark the mastman and I got the spinnaker out of the bag and fully hoisted pretty smartly. But back in the cockpit, it looked like they were having a silly-string fight. There was rope everywhere, and no one seemed to have the slightest idea what was going on. Victory looked less of a certainty.

Not that it mattered. After a boisterous start to the day, the wind slowly died. Eventually we were wallowing under slack sails that just hung from the mast. When the breeze did pick up, it came from precisely the opposite direction – genoa up, spinnaker down, rope spaghetti – then it died too. One by one, the boats around us gave up and started their engines. We hung on a bit longer, but after half an hour or so we, too, admitted defeat. Round one to the swirling winds of Loch Fyne.

Showered and changed, I went out to party like it was 1989. The names of Tarbert's pubs had been the back-drop to so many stories that I knew them by heart – the Victoria, the Islay Frigate, the Cornerhouse, the Anchor and the Tarbert Hotel. The *Moorish Idol* crew were meeting in the Victoria, at the far end of the village.

I walked there in about two minutes. Tarbert is small – some years ago a friend of Dad's, going there for the first time, asked if someone could sketch him a map. Amid much hilarity, a napkin was produced, and a single straight line was drawn on it.

The village looked much the same as it had done on my student trip. There were some sponsor's banners about, for 'Bell Lawrie Asset Management',[12] which were

---

[12] Presumably aimed at people whose assets run to more than a rusty car and a bad-tempered cat.

new, but that was about it. When I'd driven down the hill above the village the day before, the view over the harbour and its forest of slender masts had given me the same chill of excitement that it had the last time, when I'd arrived on the bus from Glasgow.

Back then, the wall of the Victoria was where a drunken group of us had decided that we'd make a human pyramid, an ambitious 4–3–2–1 affair. I was half of the 2, standing in mid-air on shaking shoulders, trying to lean enough weight against the wall to keep me up there. The most dangerous moment was when Robert, one of Dad's crew, set out for the summit.

Ignoring my father's cry of 'Don't do it, Robert! I don't mind losing a son, but you're a friend!' he clambered up, taking his purchase on belts, shoulders and the odd beard, like a superannuated Jack making the best of a reunion tour with an elderly, gin-breathing beanstalk. Astonishingly, he managed to make the summit, but found he was facing towards the wall, not outwards towards a potentially adoring public. If you stand with your face to a wall, and both feet tight to the skirting board, you'll find it's very hard to turn round without taking a step backwards. In Robert's case, the step backwards was into clean, clear Scottish air.

This all came back to me as I stood on pretty much the spot where Robert landed, where we had held our pints behind our backs and sworn to the paramedics that he'd just tripped on the step.

That wasn't even the last injury that night. Stefan was the bowman on Dad's boat. Australian, rather slight, but very strong, he was a classic cool-bowman. He could climb anywhere on the boat – up shiny aluminium masts, even up skinny, slippery synthetic ropes. He could drink his bodyweight in gin without any impairment of performance. And he was laconic in the way that drives those of us cursed with a garrulous nature into a fury. I once watched him carefully tie a sail-tie to the lifelines of the bow area, for no apparent reason. I asked him what it was for. He looked at me, paused for several seconds, then said simply, 'In case I need it.'

I would have idolised Stefan if I hadn't found him quite so intimidating. He chased sex with a dedication that made him stand out even among yachties. What really mystified me was how often he seemed to succeed, achieving results within what seemed like minutes. Certainly it was a contrast with my 'charming' approach, which took months to yield results, and only if you called 'It's nice to have a male friend who's not fixated on sex' a result.

On the night I'm talking about, Stefan was engaged in just such a quest. It involved climbing a high fence. My speculation would be that he was making an escape, although it's not impossible that he was saving some kittens from a burning building. The fence had tall spikes. Stefan slipped and, trying to save himself, put a spike through his hand. That's all the way through, and out the other side. He had to lift his weight with the other hand to get free before climbing down the fence and running off into the night. He turned up at breakfast the following morning white-faced, and with a hole in his hand.

It was stitched up without anaesthetic over bacon and eggs by a doctor, known universally as The Doctor, The Bastard – a pseudonym designed to reduce the risk of his identity becoming widely known and hence his hospital finding out where he was while he was off sick. It was clearly a matter of great pride to Stefan that he shouldn't make a sound, so we could see how hard he was. The rest of us ate noisily and enthusiastically so the other yachties eating in the hotel could see how cool we were.

Stefan had a bad week. The following night he was arrested. We didn't see what happened, we just noticed him climbing meekly into the back of a police car behind the Cornerhouse. As a drunk first-year law student (the worst kind), I marched over and demanded, 'Under what provisions are you making this arrest?'

The copper thought about this for a moment, then said, 'Piss off, son, or I'll smack you one. Are we clear?'

We were quite clear. It was a rather elegant demonstration of the difference between the theory of law and the practice. I decided to stick to the theory.

Stefan returned for breakfast in the morning. He muttered something about 'indecent exposure', which, if it was what he'd been arrested for, seemed a bit unlikely. Certainly no charges ever resulted. It hadn't been a wasted night, since he'd met a woman outside Campbelltown police station, who'd given him a bed for the night, and a lift back up the Mull to Tarbert. He arrived in time for racing, squeezed into a rhinestoned denim jacket he'd borrowed from her, which he wore all day on the foredeck in preference to his oilskins.

This kind of thing seemed to happen when you went sailing, and especially in Tarbert. Tarbert was where, a few years before, Uncle Norman, the hard-livin' hairdresser, had turned up with a crew composed of serving members of the SAS. (God knows how or why.) One of Dad's crew spilled an elite forces' pint in the

Tarbert Hotel one night, and was unwise enough to argue that the bulk of the blame lay with the positioning of the pint on the very edge of the table.

He was pursued for many hours across Tarbert and far beyond, scaling garden walls, crashing through washing-lines, tripping over gnomes and scaring sleeping sheep. He arrived, scratched and muddied, at breakfast. 'Those boys are trained killers!' he gasped. I remember, even at the time, being troubled that the SAS had been given the slip by a drunk dentist.

These things never happened to me. And you have no idea how much I wanted them to. I wanted to fit in, but I was just too well behaved. I couldn't do it. Meanwhile, my father saw the guys he sailed with as a raffish bunch of good-natured hooligans, and me as a slightly geeky son. I felt like such a disappointment – all the more so when finally I made it to Tarbert, and managed nothing more exciting than a walk-on part as an asshole law student. I'd spent so long with this double-think that I could do it myself: I'd have done anything to get arrested, as long as it didn't involve getting into trouble.

I was not in much danger of getting arrested with the *Moorish Idol* crew. We had a few civilised drinks, and went to find some fish and chips. One of us even held the door open for another customer at the fish and chip shop. We went back to the Victoria, found a table, and spent an evening telling yachtie tall tales, of gales, of breakage, of sinkings. Yachties never speak of successes, only of disasters, accompanied with urgent hand signals. All around were groups sitting around tables, taking it in turns to tell stories they'd all heard before, identical in every detail, except that last time they'd happened to someone else. It was nice, but it was dull, and it was all there seemed to be.

Gery wasn't with us for the following day's races. He and Glen had decided, and I wouldn't want to reinforce any unjustified stereotypes about sailing and money here, to take Glen's helicopter to St Andrews for lunch, and perhaps a round of golf. Apparently the weather was nicer on the east coast. They could do this without feeling guilty – they were only on *Moorish Idol* in the first place because Gery's own boat had been damaged the week before the event.

At least that explained just what they were doing with us. But their departure left us short of crew, and shorter still of talent. It didn't help that for day two we had a strong wind, gusting to over 35 knots. Neil, the boat's owner, took the helm, and while he knew what he was doing, he wasn't Gery. We had a terrible start; a dreadful first beat. We were last to the first mark, and last down the run. Then at the second mark, improbably it got worse.

'OK, guys,' shouted Neil, 'let's lose it . . . ready . . . drop!'

Without Gery and Glen, we were very short of crew to pull the spinnaker into the boat; in fact, we had just two: the mastman and me. We weren't enough. About two-thirds of the sail was still in the air when Neil turned the boat upwind at the mark. The full strength of the wind caught the sail, and that was more than two people could cope with.

I let go before I was pulled off the boat.

'I cannae hold it!' cried the mastman, a little

melodramatically, and let go as well. The sail blew into the sea, where it immediately filled with tons of water and stopped the boat dead.

This is the kind of humiliation that normally gets greeted with catcalls, applause and foghorns from the rest of the fleet. In our case, the rest of the fleet was so far in front they couldn't see us. But there are immutable laws of the sea, the most important of which is that if you fuck up, witnesses will come. In defiance of all that was fair and reasonable, who should arrive but Gery and Glen in the helicopter. They flew a couple of disbelieving laps of the boat, and naffed off for lunch.

The day's second race went stunningly as well. On the second windward leg we ripped the top of the mainsail. One of the fibreglass battens that helped shape the sail wedged itself in the rigging. That meant we couldn't continue racing, because we couldn't trim the sail. Nor could we get the sail down without wrecking it, because the batten would tear an even bigger hole.

The only way to fix this was for someone to climb the mast and remove the batten. Despite pretending I hadn't noticed something amiss, and going to stand at the other end of the boat looking the other way, it became clear that that someone was going to be me. The mastman looked more cheerful than he had in the last two days at the prospect. And I'd thought we were getting on quite well.

I tied the halyard onto my harness and climbed up the first few feet of the mast, where there's lots to hang onto. After that, it's a lot less like a climbing frame, and a lot more like trying to scramble up a fireman's pole in the wrong direction. The mastman was taking most of my weight on the halyard, which at least left me with some spare energy for hanging onto the mast. If I let go I'd be left swinging around on the end of the rope like a human wrecking-ball. Or perhaps that's a human-wrecking ball. The swinging would be fine, but I'd eventually crash into the mast, and that would hurt – I mean accident and emergency department hurt. Losing my grip didn't bear thinking about.

Every yachtie has a favourite bar story of an idiot who let go of the mast, broke every bone in his body and spent the next two days gaffer-taped to a bunk because the skipper wouldn't retire from the race. Most of them have no idea just how hard it can be to hang on. Going upwind, as we were, the mast doesn't sway, it jerks and whips as the boat hits waves, and the wind roars in your ears. By the time I was halfway to where I was going, my forearms were burning and my fingers were cramping up.

It probably took less than a minute to climb the 50 feet to the batten. It felt longer. Holding myself in the shaking rigging with my knees, I tried to ease the batten out of the sail. It was firmly wedged. I clipped myself on so I could use both hands properly, and got bashed by the mast. I had to cut away part of the batten pocket before I finally managed to remove the batten, several feet of bendy fibreglass.

I signalled down to the guys on the deck. Now that I looked, they seemed a long way away. I wanted the job done and to get back down. The mastman eased the halyard, and I held on as best I could.

I was weak-kneed in the most literal sense when I landed back on deck. It is necessary, however, to be cool.

'No problems,' I said, and grinned. I turned round

before untying the halyard from my harness, so no one could see that my hands were shaking.

Just for a moment I was transported back to an occasion from early childhood. I'd been taken on a race of some sort. There was a problem getting the spinnaker down, and a friend of Dad's climbed up to free it. I hadn't previously known this was even possible. When he came down, I gazed at him with what must have been naked adoration. It was the most swashbuckling thing I'd ever seen. He catapulted himself from dentist to superhero.[13]

The problem with this being cool is that everyone else is cool right back. Apart from a 'Cheers!' from the owner, no one said anything much at all. What I needed was an eight-year-old to worship me, someone whose lack of laid-back meant I'd be able to say, 'Yeah, no problem, part of the job. A bit rough today, but nothing I can't cope with.' I had to make do with knowing that the kid I once was would have thought I glittered like a god. I was worried that that might be narcissism.

I gave the *Moorish Idol* crew the slip that night, and went in search of excitement and excess. I did the rounds of the pubs, several times, and slipped in and out of a few conversations. There was a tent on the quay, with a bar at one end and a band at the other. The band worked its way unheeded through a medley of 1980s hits while yachties in matching crew jackets stood in little groups and shouted in each other's ears that it was all a bit loud.

---

[13] There used to be phenomenal numbers of dentists in the sailing world – to the extent that a dentists' journal once had a cartoon of two miners at the coalface, captioned, 'Well, my mother wanted me to be a dentist, but I simply couldn't stand sailing.'

That was all there was. By about nine o'clock I was
footsore from walking from pub to tent to pub. I hadn't
seen anyone barfing in the gutter. No one had passed out,
no one was waiting for an ambulance. No one was
organising sprint races from one pub to another for
money, and no one was screwing a local teenager against
the back wall of the Tarbert Hotel.

Certainly there was no one hanging by a perforated
hand from a fence. Or getting arrested – I even stopped a
pair of passing policemen and asked. 'Ach, no. Very
quiet. Not like the old days. We're only here because we
feel we ought to be.' We ended up chatting for quite a
while, because there was nothing else for either them or
me to do.

I had to finally accept that I was going to find none of
the things I was looking for. This wasn't the Tarbert I
dreamed about. Not any more.

The whole idea of going sailing had had a lot to do
with feeling that I was getting to the point in life where,
if I wasn't old, I was no longer really young. I could tell
because my twenty-two-year-old hairdresser had started
calling me 'young man'.

But almost nothing I've ever done has made me feel
quite as old as walking along the main street in Tarbert
looking for a Wild West that had gone. I didn't recognise
anyone – and it wasn't *that* long since I'd have been able
to wend my way from pub to pub and known a dozen
people in each of them. OK, all of them would have
thought, 'Hey, look, it's John Hutchinson's boring kid,
let's get out of here.' But at least I knew their names.

Had they all gone? Had they drunk themselves to
death? Were they all so changed I couldn't recognise

them? Was Stefan sitting in the corner of a pub, sipping a pint, and worrying about his stock options? I was thirty-two years old, and I was a time-traveller from a vanished age.

The following day's racing was rubbish. It was cold and wet and windy, and as a crew we were too few and too crap. Even having Gery back on the helm wasn't enough; though he had his moments, the rest of us kept wrecking them for him. We dropped the best-washed spinnaker in Scotland in the drink repeatedly, and as a grand finale stuffed a gybe so badly that even Gery couldn't prevent a broach.

Gery and Glen didn't join us for the last day at all. I didn't blame them. I'd flirted with the midnight flit myself. We lost one of the other crew as well, at least partly because a big broach the previous day had given her a real scare. Scaring easy didn't really fit with her professed experience. There were plenty of us who could sail badly; not all of us simultaneously claimed to have been part of a winning team in the Round Ireland Race. We were left with too few people to race properly.

But the views remained spectacular. The sides of the loch were steep, and plunged straight into the water. You could sail to within a few feet of the shore. The forests and bald rocks gave the whole place an exhilarating desolation. Gradually, as the sun finally came out and lit up the spinnakers, it became the best day's sailing we had at Tarbert. All pretence of racing was gone, and I was cruising on Loch Fyne again, just like the first time I'd seen the place. I even saw the funny side of being part of the worst crew Gery Trentesaux had ever sailed with. Or maybe I was just happy to be going home. Being happy to get out of Tarbert was one of the most contradictory emotions I've ever felt.

Sitting on the rail, I had a moment of therapeutic clarity. I think it was because I'd let go. I'd got it all wrong. I saw that I'd come here almost entirely because I had thought that, at last, I could catch up on all the good times that Dad and his mates had been having here throughout my childhood. I was trying to defuse a resentment that I'd been nurturing most of my life, and I was pissed off that Tarbert hadn't stood still and waited for me to come back. I didn't want this to be *like* the 1980s, I wanted it to *be* the 1980s. It had gone about as well as I should have expected.

I could live with that – it was just the result of a thirty-year sulk. What was harder was that no sooner had I had the great idea of going back to sailing than I had rapidly picked up all the old baggage that I thought I'd left behind. After many years of being a grown-up, at least some of which hadn't been a complete disaster, I'd come back to Tarbert and spent five days running up and down the main street from pub to pub trying to find some piss-heads to get into trouble with, just to prove that I could actually do irresponsibility. I hadn't managed to go back to 1980s Tarbert, but I did seem to have achieved 1980s me. Just what I'd been aiming for, except exactly the wrong way round.

We finished the race. At least, I think we did. It's possible we just retired and headed straight for Tarbert, because it didn't really matter any more. *Moorish Idol* and the rest of the crew were going straight home to Inverkip marina, so rather than go into the harbour, I jumped ashore at the first jetty we came to, and they turned and headed back to sea.

Standing to wave goodbye, I remembered standing in almost exactly the same place as a child, holding a tiny fish proudly for the camera. I smiled, because I remembered Mum taking it to the galley, and miraculously turning it into a meal for all seven of us. It was nice to reflect that thinking Tarbert would be just the same as it had been was not the stupidest thing I'd ever believed.

Chapter Seven

Tintin

AFTER TARBERT, I DIDN'T SAIL FOR SEVERAL WEEKS. It was just the way things worked out. I'd come home slightly disappointed in myself for having had such unrealistic expectations, and this matured into moderate depression about the whole idea of 'going back' to sailing. That was the problem right there: 'going back'. Everyone knows you can't go back, to anywhere or anything or anyone. 'You can't go home again.' 'You can't step in the same river twice.' 'Exact colour match cannot be guaranteed; if several tins are required mix before painting.' If Dulux can't make the same paint twice, what chance do the rest of us have? And if I couldn't go back, how on earth was I going to go forward, to the now rather silly-seeming pro dreams I'd had when the year began?

And it wasn't just Tarbert. Everything had been measured against history, and given the daydream-enhanced quality of the history involved, it wasn't surprising that reality had not measured up.

That's not to say I'd blocked out everything bad that had ever happened. Having sailing on my mind once again meant that in idle moments my memory sometimes spat out toe-curling events that I had managed to repress for years – like the occasion when I got port confused with starboard and crashed my dinghy into the club commodore's boat. This was an act of such unspeakable stupidity that instead of mercilessly taunting me for the next hundred years, the rest of the teenage sailors were just too embarrassed to mention it. Despite the regularity with which this kind of thing popped into my head, I hadn't used them as a reference. I treated them as aberrations, and airbrushed them out of my memory by working out a way in which it had all been someone else's fault. It's called editing history, and without it I don't think I could get up in the morning.

It probably helped that these few weeks coincided with cycling's national championship time-trialling season. I had planned to retire after the Commonwealth Games, but ended up going on into the UK domestic season. I was still pretty fit, and felt like going bike racing, so I did. I think maybe if the sailing had been going better, I might not have bothered.

It did me good. A few weeks of giving my attention to bike racing stopped me dwelling on the sailing disappointments. If I'd had too much time to think about sailing, I'd probably have had a fit of the sulks and given up again. As it was, by the time I got a text out of the blue, from Beth of *Afterglow*, I'd stopped being just quite such an arsehole about it.

The text said, 'Do u want 2 do crk?'

No, I didn't – and I was halfway through an irate reply

about drugs and cyclists and some of the assumptions
people make, when I twigged she didn't mean 'crack',
she meant 'Cork'.

I had to say yes. Cork Week is one of the biggest
regattas in the British Isles, and probably the best. It
wasn't just that, though. Weeks previously, when I'd
found out that *Afterglow* was going, I'd embarked on a
nagging campaign of truly pre-teen proportions. I had
bombarded poor Beth with emails, texts and calls. I even
mimed opening a wine bottle at her as our respective
boats milled about before an event on the Solent. She
didn't get it; she thought I was proposing some arresting
new sexual perversion, and gave me a cheery thumbs-up,
with embarrassing consequences all round in a Cowes
pub later that evening. Now, just when I was feeling half-
hearted, she said yes. I couldn't possibly send back a
message saying, 'No, thanks.'

Like Tarbert, I had Cork previous. Unlike Tarbert,
that previous included more than just a few days on the
set. I actually went to the very first Cork Week, in 1986.
Granted, I didn't so much race as hang out with Mum for
a week of cafés, craft shops and bracing cliff-top walks
while Dad was sailing, but I was there, and in the
evenings I got to sit in the corner of the Royal Cork
Yacht Club bar drinking Coke and eating Monster
Munch. As far as family sailing holidays went, it was
probably a better idea than the Tarbert cruise.

I went to the next event as well, at a slightly more
worldly fourteen. Originally I'd just been on the manifest
as a hanger-on, but when we got to Cork we found that
a 26-footer from Belfast Lough was short a crew-
member, and someone suggested me. I don't think the

other three realised my age until I presented myself on the dock the next morning, but they didn't mention it. I thought they were being polite – it wasn't long before I concluded that they didn't mention anything.

They communicated by telepathy. Racing-boats run on commands, most of them handed down through centuries of sailing. 'Ready about!' meaning, 'Would you be good enough to make ready for a tack?' Followed by 'Lee-ho!' – 'Tacking now.' There was none of this on *Tintin*. The helmsman just turned the boat, and the others were always ready for it. I was left scrambling to catch up. It was the same for every other manoeuvre. There wasn't even any kind of tactical discussion, or panicky shouts if anything threatened to go wrong. It was like sailing with Kraftwerk.

All that concentration and slick teamwork got results. We won the first race I did with them, and the second. They let me back onto the boat every morning, so they must have quite liked me, and after we crossed each day's final finish-line they silently handed me one of the four tins of lukewarm lager that had spent the day sitting in the plastic basin that passed for a galley sink. The noise of tins being opened sounded like gunfire. We ended the week finishing second overall in a very competitive class, which was probably the highlight of my sailing career in pure result terms. But all I remember is the silence. They didn't even say goodbye.

Item one on the *Afterglow* to-do list was to get the boat to Cork. No one wants to do the trips that shift boats from one racing venue to another. They involve taking more time off work, for a start, and more time living armpit to armpit with a group of people selected for their sailing ability rather than the unimpeachability of their personal hygiene. So delivery trips are used as a sort of penance for those who are dispensable or young or annoying. I used to do a lot of them. As a newcomer to the *Afterglow* team, and with several offences of nagging to be taken into account, it was no surprise that I got a call-up for the trip to Cork.

Six of us set out from Fowey in Cornwall on a July evening, just as daylight was dimming into blue. It was still hot from an afternoon that had seen the local beaches thronged, and those of us who drove over from Southampton baking in the car. As we hoisted the sails, the sun's glow finally faded and left a very bright full moon. The moonlight glittered on the dark waves, and there was a nice breeze from just the right direction.

It felt like a night with a punch-line coming, like the opening montage from an episode of *Casualty*. One of us should have been struck by a falling chainsaw (it's always a chainsaw), or we should have been run down by a super-tanker.[14] But neither of these things happened; it was just a beautiful night for a sail, quiet and sensual in a way that hardly makes sense on land. In two watches of three, we swapped steering, sail trimming, and making coffee.

At dawn, we were off Land's End, perfectly positioned to watch the sun rise against an indigo backdrop above the Land's End Hotel. We sniggered at the thought of

[14] There is a story from several years ago about a solo transatlantic sailor who, in very thick fog in mid ocean and seemingly miles from anyone, heard a rumbling, and had a still-lit cigarette butt land on his head. As he put it, 'You can't flick a cigarette butt very far.'

anyone who'd paid for a room, and who was peacefully asleep while one of the best views they would ever have seen unfolded on the other side of the curtains. I'm sorry to sound smug, but I'm afraid that's the reality of it. We were insufferable, but at least we were all in the same boat.

We hoisted a spinnaker, and spent the next twelve hours scorching across the Celtic Sea at 11 knots, taking it in turns to steer, competing to see who could clock up the fastest speed by catching a wave and surfing six tons of boat down it just right. When the excitement got to be too much, you could sleep in the sun, with the warm breeze blowing over your face. After no more than a few hours I felt as if I was with a group of old friends.

This was a delivery trip like none I'd been on before. In my previous experience, the sails stay stowed, and a glum, put-upon-feeling crew motored wherever they were going. Since I did most of my sailing in the Thatcherite era, when sleeping was profoundly unfashionable, watch systems were eschewed, and everyone just sat coldly in the cockpit for however many days it took the autopilot to get wherever it was going. If there was no autopilot, the youngest member of crew steered until he fell asleep, then was woken up and steered some more.

The only time I can remember a sail being hoisted was going home from Cork Week in 1992, when we had made a miscalculation with the diesel, but had a strong following wind. I was (shamefully) asleep down below in the middle of the night when I was woken by an almighty bang and the ceiling smacking me in the face. Given that our navigator was only about halfway through *Learn Navigation in a Weekend*, I assumed we'd hit something

(Ireland sprang to mind), and were perhaps already sinking. As the boat came upright, I bolted up the companionway steps onto the deck complete with life raft, ready to abandon ship.

A dozing helmsman had let the boat gybe, and then broach. One of the crew had had his head cracked open by the boom sweeping across the deck, which produced an astonishing amount of blood. We patched him up in the dark as best we could, and dropped him ashore at first light in Dunmore East, on the south-east corner of Ireland, to find himself medical treatment as best he could, and some means of getting home.

We bought some diesel, and motored all the way to Belfast Lough, most of two days, with no food, since no one had thought to buy any. The only sustenance was a case of tonic water. We'd have been almost immune to malaria and muscle cramps, but as silver linings went, its value was undermined by the freezing temperatures and pouring rain.

That felt like a very long time ago. *Afterglow*'s sail to Cork was magical – it was beyond that, and into miraculous. I'd set off with doubts about the whole idea of sailing, what I was doing and why I was doing it. It was the beautiful counterpoint to Tarbert, where my high expectations had been followed by the deep, penetrating disappointment of realising I'd been so wrong about so much. Now, where I'd expected nothing apart from a sulky couple of days motoring across to Cork with a bunch of strangers, I'd had one of the best sails of my life.

In common with many parents of the 70s and 80s, mine often drew my attention to what they regarded as the best attributes of my friends, to encourage me to improve my own generally lacklustre performance. In their eyes, the perfect son had the handwriting of Mark Harris, the manners of Ian McNeil, and the intellectual acumen of Stephen McGuire. They didn't seem to feel that having to cherry-pick across several different children might suggest they were setting the bar unreasonably high. Nor did they think it relevant that Mark Harris's lovely penmanship accompanied a level of intelligence so low that he couldn't tell the difference between his packed lunch and his underpants.[15] The predictable result of all this was that I developed a dislike for most of my friends.

Most lacking of all was the sunny, open disposition of Patrick Walsh, youngest son of a local farming family. I hated him anyway. One of my earliest memories is of Patrick upstaging me at my fourth birthday party by arriving atop some absurdly large piece of bright-red agricultural machinery, with the air of one who'd just knocked off from a hard day's work. I was inarticulate with rage. The day his family moved to Dublin was the happiest of my life.

Then, when I was sixteen, during another delivery trip to Cork, we stopped at Dunmore East. Patrick turned up in a pub, on holiday with some schoolmates, assured, cool and still metaphorically sitting on a combine harvester. Before I knew where I was, he'd usurped my position as everyone's favourite teenager. He told jokes and bought drinks with casual sophistication. And he decided he'd like to come to Cork with us, not to sail, just for the drinking. I could barely contain my delight.

---

[15] No, we couldn't believe it either.

At least he hadn't pushed me out of the crew itself. 'Ha!' I thought. 'Let's see how smart you look standing on the dock as we all sail off every morning in our matching shirts.' An empty hope. Patrick could find a way of demonstrating his laid-back style under any circumstances. We hadn't been in Cork longer than a day before I desperately wanted him to go sailing, and me to stand on the dock.

Patrick got kicked out of his bunk on the boat each morning when we left to go racing. And each morning he transplanted his sleeping arrangements to a plum spot on the lawns in front of the Royal Cork Yacht Club. Like Top Cat, complete with eye-mask and earplugs, he slept for most of the day while a fretful sub-committee of club members stood nearby, wondering what to do about him. Such a liberty had never been taken before, and thus a precedent did not exist. In any event, they weren't allowed to walk on the lawn. This debate was carried out in a murmur, because Patrick commanded respect even when he was asleep. They had to be careful not to wake him.

Early each afternoon, Patrick got up, rolled up his sleeping bag, and went to the members-only showers to wash, and gel his elegant coiffure into place. The sub-committee dispersed, reassuring each other that he wouldn't come back the next day. By the time we came in from racing, Patrick was well rested, and prepared for another night's partying.

But, damn him, it didn't end there. It's traditional, or it was, for the youngest member of crew to be custodian of the drink kitty. It means you spend half your life going to the bar, queuing for many minutes, then trying to carry ten pints back to the party. After I'd completed one such epic, Patrick said, 'I'll go next time. There has to be an easier way than that.'

Next time, Patrick took the kitty, and disappeared. He was back a very few moments later, empty-handed. 'Ha!' I thought, again. Seconds later, a teenage barman arrived with a tray of drinks and a sycophantic attitude.

'Turns out young Peter here and I have some previous,' announced Patrick, putting his arm round the barman's shoulders. 'I'm his prefect back at school. Isn't that right, Peter?'

Peter grinned nervously.

'Somehow, I feel confident he'll look after us *very* well this week.'

All further trips to the bar consisted of catching Peter's eye. He dropped whatever he was doing and came running. It would have been a brilliantly satisfactory arrangement if it had been brokered by anyone but Patrick. I could see my father looking from me to Patrick and back to me. And I could see him sigh in disappointment.

By the time I arrived on *Afterglow*, Patrick's lawn had vanished under a beer tent, which I think he would have approved of. The beer tent wasn't the only one. There were food tents, innumerable shop tents, sailmakers' tents, at least two chandlery tents, a tent for a band, and a folk music tent that at no point all week contained anything other than two middle-aged guitar-playing beards working their way through a version of 'The Fields of Athenry' that was even more endless than usual.

There were flags, banners and alfresco dining areas. Even on Saturday, two days before the racing started, the place was thronged. And there was a PA announcer with a terribly posh Irish accent who sounded like she was being handed the announcements on small bits of paper one word at a time: 'Would . . . the . . . owner . . . of . . . car . . .'

We spent two days fixing things. Racing-yachts are, pretty much from the moment of launch, falling apart. There will never be a point where everything works.[16] Bits break regularly, normally because they are expensive and hi-tech, and consequently too flimsy, or cheap and rubbishy, and consequently too flimsy. It's usual to replace anything that breaks with something exactly the same, despite the empirical proof that the last one wasn't up to the job. This is one of the ways the marine industry makes money out of people like *Afterglow*'s owner and skipper, Dougal, who wouldn't stand for it in any other area of life.

Dougal was in his mid forties, and normally laid-back and cheerful in a manner that would have been avuncular if he'd been older. There was an element of embarrassing dad about him – he couldn't help but pull a face whenever anyone produced a camera. As a skipper, he was pretty relaxed too. He pulled rank rarely, and only when he felt someone wasn't pulling their weight, or had overstepped the boundary and was trespassing on his authority. On these occasions, he gave off a quietly angry vibe that I was keen to avoid having directed at me.

---

[16] I met a naval architect who, not entirely reassuringly, said, 'All boats are sinking. It's just a matter of how fast.' Sometimes it's quite fast: at pretty much the moment the Italian America's Cup boat *Italia 2* hit the water for the first time, the crane being used for the launch fell over and sent it to the bottom of the harbour.

While the rest of us greased winches and spliced sheets, Dougal spent two full days working on a computer system that he claimed already worked. This was an impressively long time, given that his day job was as something awfully high-powered in the world of IT. It is not impossible that the system may have been over-complex, since Dougal was a gadget freak. He readily admitted that the two blank buttons on the dash of his Volvo were driving him mad: 'I got all the optional extras. But someone, somewhere, has something I don't. I lie awake nights wondering what I'm missing out on.'

Dougal's boat rather resembled Dougal himself. *Afterglow* was basically sound, but had a few idiosyncrasies. It leaked round the deck fittings, so that it needed significant bailing out after each race. The fuel gauge didn't work, so we ran out of diesel with monotonous regularity. And the top rudder bearing-housing was not properly attached, so that every so often there would be a deep bass 'thump' as it moved. I spent a long time looking at it one morning before deciding it probably wasn't going to come adrift entirely, and allow the rudder to drop off the bottom of the boat. Probably.

This kind of thing isn't unusual. Most racing-yachts fall some way short of the gin-and-tonic luxury you might expect for your several hundred thousand pounds. The cash buys hulls made from exotic composites, carbon-fibre masts, flash sails and computer systems that rarely if ever work. It doesn't get spent on making life comfortable.

When you dropped down the five steps from the companionway hatch into the cabin, there was just about standing headroom. The internal fitting was in wood veneer and white gelcoat. There was a basic galley, with a two-ring stove, and a sink with a tap that didn't work. But the sink was a good place to keep sunscreen. There were eight bunks round the main cabin and aft below the cockpit area. No normally constructed human over the age of six could get into the topmost aft bunks. If they could have it would have been exactly like sleeping in a coffin, only without all the little luxurious touches that make a coffin so welcoming.

On the opposite side of the boat from the galley was a chart table – just a desk with a lid and a laptop, surrounded by electronic readouts. It looked like the flight deck from a plywood spaceship. On the floor there were always three or four headsails, folded into sausage-shaped bags that ran the length of the main cabin, past the mast, and into the forward 'cabin', where there was a bunk that was perfectly suited to anyone who was four-feet tall and shaped like the letter 'V'. In a small phone-box-sized compartment near the mast was the heads, which in a break with racing-yacht tradition worked, and thus had not yet been superseded by a bucket. ('Bucket and chuck it' is the technical term.)

The thing is that if you'd taken her to the Boat Show when she was brand-new, without the piles of sails and tools, put a half-sliced loaf of bread on the galley and a bunch of flowers on the chart table in the traditional if surreal fashion, she'd have looked pretty good.[17] It's just that the reality of a racing-yacht's life is getting wet, being shaken, having sails constantly hauled in and out of hatches, and being lived in by an only semi-domesticated

[17] One of the boats at the Boat Show had flowers in a rubber vase. I can't help feeling that if circumstances call for a rubber vase, you probably don't need a vase at all.

bunch of sailors. I once heard a newcomer to offshore sailing complain there was nowhere to store his dirty laundry. 'You've got a whole fucking boat for dirty laundry,' was the reply.

Maybe it was just because I was still buzzing from the sail over, but I enjoyed working on the boat. I'd love to report that I performed some top-drawer light-engineering, but in reality, since I was new, I was entrusted only with cleaning the galley. My girlfriend would have watched, slack-jawed, as I set to with energy and meticulousness and polished the place until it shone. You must remember this wasn't a kitchen – this was a galley. This was man's work. I've never enjoyed cleaning so much. As long as I could forget that on deck, Ellie was stripping and greasing winches, I was fine.

It wasn't just me; across the whole marina there was an atmosphere of anticipation as other crews did the same things we were doing. There was a constant background of hammering noises, men up masts fixing things, shouts of, 'Has anyone got the big hacksaw?' and people scurrying back and forth to the chandlery tent. You couldn't make people work that hard by paying them. I'll admit to a sneaking suspicion that since a lot of these people are bankers, accountants and other such desk-based wealth-shufflers, most of them rather enjoy the macho world of taking their shirts off and hitting things with a hammer.

Life settled into an appealingly simple rhythm of working, eating, drinking, and nothing much more. We had rented a house half a mile downstream, and on the far side of the river. To get there, we had borrowed an ancient fibreglass dinghy that, frustratingly, would only hold eight of the ten crew safely. Sometimes we made two trips. Sometimes we chanced it and did it in one, with the water a few inches below the gunwales, petrified (well, I was anyway) that someone was going to roar past and swamp us in their wash.

We were in this overloaded mode one evening, paddling very gently downstream having run out of fuel in the outboard motor. As we approached the old jetty in front of the house, we saw there was a couple sitting at the end of it, involved in a reasonably advanced bit of foreplay. At least, it looked advanced to me. It was just the night for it, it was warm and still, the stars were bright, and music drifted across the dark water from the club. In fact, it must have been lovely for them, right up to the point where ten pairs of eyes slid silently to a viewing position three feet away.

'Ha-umm,' said Dougal, by way of an icebreaker. The couple jumped.

'Sorry to spoil the mood,' said Ellie.

'Should we ask them to take a mooring line?' said someone, in a stage whisper.

'It's not as if he doesn't have anything to tie it to,' said Beth.

They were a good bunch, and for the first time all year I felt like part of a team. It was great.

When the racing started, I was tasked with minding the downhaul, a very simple job, at which I was utterly terrible. All I had to do was obey basic instructions. I was worse at this than you would believe possible. I spent my time gazing about, looking at other boats, and trying to second-guess the tactics. Meanwhile, Beth would say something like, 'Guy back . . . downhaul off . . . down-haul off . . . DOWNHAUL! . . . MICHAEL! ...' On my old Mirror, this job was done by a bit of elastic, and frankly it was done much better.

Then, halfway through the first race on day three, this happened: 'Michael,' said Ben, the tactician and Dougal's second in command, 'Liz isn't feeling great. Could you come back and do her side of the cockpit for a while?'

So Liz and I swapped places. The job was barely more technical, but it had a grander name: I was now 'trimmer 2'. When we tacked, I liked to think that years of experience allowed me to whip the sheet off the winch with a practised flick of the wrist, but to be honest just letting it go would have done. It wasn't hard.

What it did mean was that I was now within earshot of Ben and Dougal at the back of the boat. At the next start, as we sailed down the starting-line with about ten minutes to go, I said, 'So, we'll be trying for the port end of the line?' Dougal hadn't actually worked out which end of the line he wanted, and was surprised that I was right.

'But,' I continued, emboldened, 'while the wind direction is oscillating about ten degrees every six or seven minutes, it has an overall trend towards the right side of the course, so ideally we want to go right up the beat and that means not getting trapped too far out on the left side by everyone else.'

Ben and Dougal were nearly as impressed with this magnificent sentence as I was. (The last time I'd said anything like that out loud, Dobbs had replied, 'You're sailing on water, not paper, you spaz.' Then he decided 'spaz' was a bit primary school, and added, 'Asshole.')

All I meant was that the fastest way to get to the first mark would be to start at the left-hand side of the start-line, but then to try to work our way across to the right-hand side of the course. But it sounded better the way I said it.

With ninety seconds to the start, we were fighting to find a good position on a very crowded line.

'Bring her up a bit, Dougal,' said Ben. Then immediately, 'No, no, no, he's tacking, he's tacking, bear off.' Dougal turned the boat sharply, missing the other boat's stern by a couple of feet.

I was down to leeward, with a good view, and said to Ben, 'We've got space to gybe round, kill some time. We're very early.'

Ben looked for himself. 'Yep, Dougal, let's gybe round.'

Dougal paused – I wasn't sure whether he was deciding if he agreed or just making the point that he was in charge. Then he called, 'Gybing!' and spun the wheel. I liked this. They were listening to me.

Forty-five seconds to go, and we were still early, but there were quite a few boats in front of us all the same. The boats in front slowed down, trying to stay behind the line, and the boats behind kept going, producing a dense pack with incidents, a few small collisions, and vast amounts of shouting. The boat to windward started to bear down towards us, being pressured by another boat.

'Stay up! UP! ' called Dougal. There was a small bump. 'Protest!' he shouted. Another bump. 'Come on, guys, stay up!' There was a flash of anger from Dougal. The other skipper acknowledged the protest call. That meant an argument for the race judges to deal with later.

After all that, our start was mediocre – we were stuck in the scrum. It took several minutes to get some space

– some boats tacked off and things opened out a bit. Ben spotted what he reckoned was a clear lane across – where we could thread our way through the boats heading towards the left of the course, like someone sauntering across several lanes of moving traffic without breaking stride.

He was right, and it was a good call. Clear air, heading for the smart side of the beat (or what I thought was the smart side, not necessarily the same thing). If we'd had a decent start we could have pretended we were real stars. We'd have been kidding ourselves, though – real stars get a good start almost every time. Like Gery at Tarbert, all the other boats seem, magically, to get out of their way.

I concentrated on the wind – the instruments and the boat's compass heading for its exact direction, and the water for any darker, ruffled bands where a bit more breeze would be found. I tried to keep track of the pattern of the shifts, so I'd be better able to decide whether a shift was likely to be more than a fleeting variation.[18]

[18] I may as well have a crack at explaining this windshift thing properly, since it's about 50 per cent of decent race tactics. Please, honestly, feel free to ignore the following. At the start of an upwind leg, the mark you're sailing for will be directly upwind. Since you can't sail directly into the breeze, you'll be heading at something like forty-five degrees to the straight-line course to the mark. The wind can then shift. Since you sail at a constant angle to the wind, that can bring your heading closer to the straight-line course, a 'lift', or push you away, a 'header'.

The idea is to hold your course on the lifts, since you can sail closer to the direction you want to go, and tack on the headers, since a header on one tack is a lift on the other. Get it right, and you're always sailing the best angle. The difference between getting it right and wrong is significant. If the wind oscillates by five degrees every few minutes, a boat that gets it right each time is sailing at an effective angle of forty degrees. Get it wrong, and it's fifty degrees. That will gain something like 170 metres every kilometre. (Except that the way the world works means that the bastards who can spot every shift can probably do everything else better than you too, but never mind.)

'Ben, we're down about nine degrees, and we've got good breeze here,' I said. Ben looked to weather to see if there were boats in our way if we tacked. 'Still down nine, it's staying constant,' I said.

'Dougal, he's right, let's take a tack,' said Ben. We did, and we gained ground. I felt rather pleased with myself.

This was how we worked the beat – I watched the wind and talked to Ben, Ben watched the other boats and talked to Dougal, trying to reconcile the demands of the shifts with the positions and wind-shadows of the boats around us. Dougal tried to balance the single-mindedness needed to steer the boat fast, watching the sails and the waves, with looking around to see whether or not he agreed with Ben.

Between us we got it about right. I called one shift wrongly, where the wind just shifted back after we tacked, and on another occasion we were blocked by another boat, something we could have avoided with more foresight. But overall, we had a good leg, and a decent race. We finished in mid-fleet thanks to the start, but all we had to do was kid ourselves that next time we'd get the start we deserved (but were, as things turned out, serially incapable of achieving), and we'd be unstoppable.

Ben and Dougal seemed happy enough that I'd stuck my uninvited oar into their decision-making. I got moved back to the cockpit for the rest of the week. 'You called some nice shifts – keep doing it,' said Ben. I tried not to look too pleased. It's worth mentioning, I think, that this was the first time, ever, ever-ever-ever, that anyone had complimented me for something tactical on a boat.

No amount of cleverness would have helped the

following day. Unlike most of the week's racing – which was round short courses marked with big inflatable marks – this was a longer race of five or six hours. At the first mark, after about an hour and a half of racing, we were doing well, by our standards.

Then the wind dropped, and a cold, drizzly fog rolled in. We inched on towards the next mark. The leg took two hours, at an average speed of about 1 knot, and most of that was tide. When we got there, and had to turn round, we stopped completely. And so did everyone else. All of us sat in a clump near the mark, in the drizzle, and waited for wind. And waited.

'Guys,' said Ben, 'I hate to say this, but we've just been overtaken by a butterfly.'

Indeed. It fluttered by, thundering towards the finish. We, in our £100,000 yacht, watched it jealously. Some jellyfish passed us too. The sails flopped about as the boat wallowed in the Atlantic rollers. The instrument readouts showed, to two decimal places, that there was no wind, and we weren't moving. Tectonic plates could go faster. At this rate, we'd be lucky to reach Crosshaven before Crosshaven reached the Urals. We sat for hours, waiting for something to happen. When the abandonment of the race was announced over the radio, there were cheers from the nearby boats.

I was quietly satisfied with how things had gone before the wind ran out. Once again I'd been right substantially more often than I'd been wrong. Dougal and Ben may not have had total faith in everything I said, but they certainly seemed to reckon I was worth listening to.

I'll be honest. I was beginning to have doubts about whether I'd always been as crap at this as I remembered.

I thought that the information and opinions I was feeding back to Ben and Dougal was pretty basic stuff – stuff that pretty much anyone I was racing Mirrors with at Carrickfergus would have needed to be on top of. But while it wasn't anything that Ben and Dougal didn't know about, it wasn't so simple that they could do it without thinking about it. Having me do it clearly helped.

This was a shock. A lack of competence was something I'd long accepted. It was supported by a considerable weight of evidence, and dozens of witnesses. I'd resigned myself to it – most of the idea of taking up sailing again was to see just what had kept me hammering away for years at something I couldn't do. Now, it appeared, I could do it after all. While this was not a disappointment as such, it still pulled the rug from under things rather.

Or, to be exact, I could do part of it. I was one-third of able-to-do-it-after-all. One-third, on a boat heading for mid-fleet mediocrity, a boat that in my teenage years I'd have dismissed as making up the numbers. I was still pleased about it.

Here's the thing: racing a sailing boat well is very difficult, I've always known that. But I don't think that was my problem. As a dinghy sailor, I was never good enough to get as far as finding what I was doing difficult. I got stuck at complicated. It was all just a blur. Here is a brief guide to all the things you have to do when you're helming a dinghy on an upwind leg.

1. Watch the headsail, and the tufts of wool or ribbon (tell-tales) that show just how the wind is flowing over the sail, and keep them flying by holding the

correct angle to the wind. This is a matter of steering just a degree or two each way.

2. Watch for waves – hitting a big wave badly can stop the boat almost dead, and the smaller ones will knock you off the course determined by point 1.

3. Watch the compass, not for the heading, but to see where the wind is taking you and judge the shifts. Remember the compass headings, and their ranges, and any overall trends, on each tack.

4. Consider the effects of tides, which will generally be stronger in deeper water.

5. Watch the water to look for gusts and lulls, tailoring your steering to take advantage.

6. Trim the mainsail, using the five ropes available for the purpose. At least one of these (the sheet) will need adjustment almost constantly to deal with the gusts and lulls you saw coming under point 5.

7. Watch all the other boats. Are you likely to hit any of them and, if so, will it be your fault? Where are they going? How fast are they going? What are they doing that's different to you if they're going faster? Will any of them be in your way in the next few minutes? Will any of them get between you and the wind? If it's a series, where are your overall rivals?

8. Where is the next mark?

9. Cultivate a warm, loving relationship with your crew through the medium of shouting instructions and handing out blame.

10. And, for Belfast Lough sailors only, are you about to sail into a patch of shit-eating jellyfish, and, if so, is anyone near enough to chuck one down the back of your crew's neck? Can you get close enough?

Now, almost any one of these was beyond me. Do it all together? What do you think?

If you can dinghy well, you can do anything. Ben Ainslie, who is a better sailor than I can possibly even describe, said that not long after the start of a race he can look at the boats and the water, feel what the wind is doing, and see in his mind the pattern of the race, and how it must play itself out. This is beyond my comprehension. Not only do I not understand how he does it, I don't understand how it can even be possible.

If you don't have this kind of profound, and I suspect substantially instinctive, understanding, it all becomes a bit much. I could never hold enough of it in my head at once to start worrying about patterns. If I'd had any sense I'd have tried hard to learn them one at a time – start off with steering and not crashing, then wind, then tactics. I'd have avoided entirely worrying about weird stuff I'd read in books, like the way the wind swerves depending on the roughness of the surface it's blowing over.

But that would have required a level of patience from the twelve-year-old me that I haven't achieved today. After all, just a couple of months before Cork Week, I'd come back to sailing expecting, first, to pick up where I'd left off, and, second, to move swiftly on to the fulfilment of ambitions that had eluded me last time. Then I'd quickly become really pissed off when it didn't all work out immediately. Yup, a totally different person.

No, I'd wanted to be good immediately and I felt like a real failure when I wasn't a natural genius. I was, I think, rather hard on myself. My dinghy mediocrity proved nothing more than that I was never going to be brilliant, but that's not quite the same thing as being crap. It just felt like that.[19]

The reason I was doing well on *Afterglow* was precisely because, finally, twenty-something years too late, I was only trying to worry about one bit, wind. Dougal did the steering, and Ben did the rest of it. It's not irrelevant that despite several years skippering his own boats, Dougal still steered best when he had nothing else to worry about.

The day after the coastal race threw further light on this matter of slicing the jobs up. That's because it was the horrendous, hungover aftermath of an appallingly drunken night, where we'd hit, alternately, the hard liquor and the dance floor until 2 a.m. Then we'd taken a terrifying trip downriver to our rented house in the overloaded fibreglass rowing boat, during which I was so certain we were all going to die that I kept one hand on my phone and the other on my life-jacket inflation toggle – at least in my last few minutes alive I'd be buoyant enough to enjoy the coast-guard's switchboard playing 'Greensleeves' at me. ('Your survival is important to us; please hold the line, and one of our operators will be with you shortly.') When, miraculously, we got to the house, we drank everything in it.

By the following morning Dougal had gone grey, and was hanging limply off the wheel. He could only just steer, let alone muster much independent thought. Ben could just blearily make out enough other boats to tell Dougal if he was going to crash into anyone.

---

[19] I have, of course, another way of looking at this. I *am* a terrific cyclist (or at any rate I was). Every so often I get persuaded to do talks at bike clubs, and one of the questions that always comes up is, 'How do you pace a time-trial effort evenly across the whole race?' I don't really have an answer. I just can. I could do it the first time I tried, and I have no idea how.

Miraculously, I was still able to remember that compass heading numbers get bigger as you turn right, so I could still work out which way the wind was blowing. But talking made my head hurt, so I didn't say anything unless I had to. It was the same for everyone else. We concentrated on our own jobs, and let everyone else do theirs. It was as quiet as it had been on *Tintin* in 1988.

For the crew of *Afterglow* it was a revolution – there had been races where we had seemed more like a debating society than a sports team. We got easily our best result of the series, a tenth. Maybe Stephen Dobbs and I should have drunk more.

My last Cork Week before giving up was in 1992. Uncharacteristically, I don't remember much about it. I think maybe my heart wasn't really in it. I do recall that due to leaving things a bit late we spent the week living in one of several small caravans that some local entrepreneur had parked in a steep, muddy field behind the club. It rained. It blew. The caravan leaked and rocked in the wind, until it was an exact simulation of the boat we were all trying to avoid having to sleep in. I decided that the boat would do me fine after one particularly traumatic night in the caravan spent pretending to be asleep (and not jealous) while one of the crew shagged a local girl who made a noise like a squeaky toy when she got excited. Or maybe it was him; like I said, I had my eyes closed so tight I got cramp in my eyelids.

Of the sailing itself, I can dig up almost nothing, despite being part of a crew several of whom were in the final stages of preparing for the Barcelona Olympics. The strongest image I have comes not from memory, but from a photograph that hangs on my parents' kitchen wall.

It's the best picture of any of the boats Dad sailed. The sea and sky are the requisite shades of blue, and the spinnaker is flying perfectly. My father is sitting at the stern, wearing an overly bright shirt that clashed with the rest of the crew kit, and a dreadful white flat-cap that he must have been given for free. I'm there as well, at the front of the cockpit, sitting in the odd, lopsided position I always seemed to be in whenever anyone took a photo of me sailing.

What gives the photo an air of drama is that instead of just a handful of other boats and a distant horizon, the background is the town of Cobh, dramatically fore-shortened by the telephoto lens, with the tall spire of the cathedral and tiers of colourful buildings apparently stacked on top of each other on a steep slope rising from the shore. This isn't a long, dull sail to nowhere in particular; this is close-quarters racing, apparently mere feet away from the shore, and it looks exciting. It hangs opposite the seat I get at the table when I'm visiting my parents. I must have spent hours gazing at it.

The photo was taken during a race around Cork Harbour, dodging the rocks and headlands, through mysterious tidal eddies understood only by the locals, and trying to avoid the wind-shadows cast by the inlet's steep sides. The rest of the week's races, on the open sea outside the headlands guarding the harbour, were fairer, but for all the reasons that make the photo so dramatic, the harbour race was always popular. And that was how *Afterglow* finished the week.

It has to be said that the atmosphere on board was a little flat – the regatta was almost over, and most of us were already contemplating a return to work. Several of the crew were looking forward to a delivery trip back to Southampton in, if the forecast was to be believed, horrible conditions.

We had recovered from the previous day's collective hangover. The debating chamber was in full cry; every time I suggested the wind had shifted, any number of voices would agree that it had, or argue that it hadn't. There would be demands from halfway up the boat that we tack to get out of another boat's dirty air, often as not at the likely cost of T-boning another boat that whoever it was couldn't see. Ellie had to trim the spinnaker through a barrage of suggestions about how she should do it, until she eventually turned and said that if any of us really thought we could do better they were welcome to do so. It didn't shut us up for long or, really, at all. The babble irritated Dougal, who got progressively grumpier as the race went on, eventually turning off most of the instrument readouts to try to give us less to talk about.

I didn't much care. The highlight of my day was obvious. I'd been looking forward to it all week. We rounded a mark just to the east of Cobh, hoisted a spinnaker, to sail west across a backdrop that I could have drawn and coloured from memory. There was even the same photographer, in the same place, to take the picture. I have the result on my kitchen wall. I'm waiting to see how many years elapse before my parents notice.

I loved Cork Week. It was everything I'd been hoping for from sailing, and of course it came along when I didn't expect it. It came along *because* I didn't expect it, which was an irritating irony. Never mind. I suppose it also helped that I'd been there before. I could remember frustrations like Patrick, or like the grotty caravan. Cork wasn't handicapped by the almost mythological status of Tarbert. It was just a place.

The things that made the week so good were not, of course, the same things that had held me captive in sailing as a teenager. When I'd gone as a teenager it had been about competition, about results and the pursuit of excellence. This had been about beer and sunshine and making friends, and other things adolescent me would have scoffed at. At Cork 2006 I only cared enough about our results for long enough to discuss them in the bar at night. Apart from our high-point of tenth, they've gone already, while results from the 1980s are all still carefully logged. When I succumb to dementia, they'll probably be the last things to slip away.

By the time my airport taxi arrived on Friday afternoon, after the harbour race, I was really very sorry to be leaving. I felt like I could maintain a pattern of sailing, drinking, sleeping for a few hours, and going sailing again indefinitely. After the blue skies of Cork, everyday life was going to seem rather bland. (Anyone familiar with the climate of south-west Ireland will appreciate that this is not a phrase that gets overused.)

But it wasn't going to be for long. Dougal had asked me to do Cowes Week, which was only a fortnight away. *Britannia*, Prince Philip, the Spiritual Home of Yachting™, and all with a bunch of people I'd come to like very much. Finally I was getting somewhere.

The postscript to Cork Week is that, instead of sailing the boat back to England, I had to fly home to get to a friend's stag weekend. Cork airport was crowded with sailors, and the flight had cost a fortune. I hauled myself through Heathrow, and across London to meet in a pub in Soho, and from there to the best man's selection of mystery venue. The mystery venue turned out to be Cork. I flew back on the same sodding plane. The cabin staff probably thought I was a drug's mule. Actually, I was just a man with really, really stupid friends.

Chapter Eight

Britannia

BY MID JULY, I HAD CALLUSES THAT MADE ME LOOK like I was holding a handful of snails, and a deep suntan on my face that stopped abruptly at collar level. I also had a bank account that, to my horror, was almost empty. I didn't know where it had gone. I hadn't exactly been loaded when I started out on my sailing journey, but I'd been all right. Not any more – for the first time since I was a student, my bank had to explain to me (rather patronisingly, I felt) that before I could take any money out, it would be necessary to put some in.

It took a day of forensic accounting to work out where it had gone. Beer, it turned out. Mainly for other people, it has to be said, but that didn't really numb the pain, it just salved my liver. Beer and hotels, the house rental in Cork, air fares, petrol, oilskins, three sorts of waterproof jacket, a fleece, a harness, boots, gloves, food, a few contributions to costs like berthing fees, train fares, ferry fares . . . After a while I gave up and accepted that I hadn't been robbed, I'd been dissolute. I also had the nagging fear that Cowes Week was not going to be a cheap way to spend the first few days of August.

There is, of course, a theory that sailing is a sport for the rich. There is some truth in this. Boats are expensive. Everything about them is expensive – sails and synthetic ropes cost more than you would believe – for a 40-foot boat, a full suit of sails could be upwards of £40,000, depending who you buy them from.

The thing is that as far as that kind of money is concerned, all the bills land with one person, the owner. To own a full-on racing-yacht is to have a bank account in free fall, and the only question is how much money you had to begin with.

Everyone else needs only enough to pay for kit and expenses. I'd run into trouble simply because I'd done too many events, and not spent enough time working in between to pay for them – for most of the *Afterglow* crew, Cork was their only big regatta of the year, just as most of *Moorish Idol*'s team were only doing Tarbert.

What skews the demographic – and where the money problem intersects with the posh problem – is that the owner calls the shots. He decides who gets to go sailing and who does not, and he (it usually is a he) finds new crew via friends, or friends of friends, or people who are members of the yacht club. If they dig them up via crew-search websites, they'll only pick those with experience, and guess how you get the experience. So while not everyone has to be well off, they tend to be resolutely middle class, white and well educated, or at any rate expensively educated.

In the course of the year, to the best of my recollection, I sailed with: a tabloid journalist, a broadsheet journalist, an ice-cream baron, a man who worked for the sex-toy department of Amazon.co.uk,[20] a GP, two naval architects, a dentist, the CEO of a large publishing company, the CEO of a steel fabricators, a viola player, two management consultants, any number of IT professionals and half a dozen people with incomprehensible jobs in the City. There were plenty of people whose occupation never came up, and quite a few students, but they all blended in seamlessly.

Not all of these people were rich; several of them were not really all that well off at all. But they all came from the same kind of background, and, frankly, none of them had ever looked down the back of the sofa for small change with which to buy lunch.

There are exceptions, of course there are. I didn't actually meet any, but they are there. They must be. Somewhere.

The hostility is about more than just middle-classness, of course. If that was it, then we'd have the BBC, the National Portrait Gallery and Stephen Fry against a wall as well. There is an assumption that there is something terribly smug and insular about sailing, or even something intrinsically nasty about the people who do it.

I've certainly come across some offensive behaviour. In 2006 I saw a group of people having a vintage champagne-spraying fight with magnums at £200 each. I was once on a boat where, passing a group of sea-anglers in a motor-boat, the skipper cried, 'Look, everyone, poor people!' and the crew yelled rapier witticisms like, 'Go

---

[20] Yup, really. Oh, and the ice-cream maker once dated a circus knife-thrower. Not really relevant, but quite interesting.

back to your council estate!' at them. I had only joined that particular crew for one race, and I didn't sail with them again.

But that's been about it. I don't think it's unique to sailing. I saw similar levels of social insensitivity while I was a student at 'posh' university in a former mining area. I don't even think it's got much to do with either poshness or money, it's got to do with being an obnoxious prick. And being an obnoxious prick is not an activity open only to the comfortably off, it's just that sailing can offer a wonderfully high-profile means of being an obnoxious prick. But I know that I'm not arguing my way out of this. It's the class system, which runs on prejudice and mutual hatred, and it seems unlikely that I'm going to bring that crashing down as a side project in a book about sailing.

What definitely doesn't help is that royal families seem inexorably drawn to the sport – King Juan Carlos of Spain sails, Queen Sofia was in the 1960 Olympic team, their son Felipe sailed and carried the Spanish flag at the 1992 Olympics in Barcelona ('Hmm, who shall we pick?'). King Harald of Norway competes at a high level, and Constantine, former King of Greece, passes the long days in exile as Honorary President of the International Sailing Federation.

Inevitably, the British royals sail. When I was growing up, press reports on Cowes Week could be relied upon to include a picture of Prince Philip standing behind the wheel of a yacht, usually wearing a hat of which my father would have been proud. The boat was invariably borrowed, since he and the Queen had sold their own racing-yacht, *Bloodhound*, in 1969.

Of course, the sale of *Bloodhound* didn't just net a few quid to help with Prince Charles's college fund (money well spent), it allowed them to spend more time with their other yacht, *Britannia*, which was for many years the traditional backdrop to Cowes Week, and in terms of race-week accommodation a substantial step up from a caravan in a muddy field.

She wasn't the first *Britannia*, just the first to so strongly resemble a 1950s channel ferry.[21] I was much more interested in the original *Britannia*, a J-class racing-yacht built in 1893 for the Prince of Wales, later Edward VII. Paintings and photographs show a long, low, dark-painted hull, with the sweetly curved lines that characterised that era of racing-yachts. I have no idea from where, but I always had very clear notions on boat aesthetics. To me, *Britannia* looked impossibly lovely.

She must have been a bastard to actually sail. The sails, all 10,000 square feet of them, were of cotton. Even when they were dry handling them would take many men. Wet, it must have been awful. One photograph taken on board shows two men in naval caps fighting the kicking wheel, their faces screwed up against the sheets of spray, up to their ankles in water running across the deck. This may have been the most elegant age yachting ever

[21] Or, as the always oleaginous Andrew Morton put it writing for *Boat International*, '[A] splendid example of contemporary British design and technology.' He went on to observe that she would often detour to post a letter, and that there was a twenty-six-piece marine band always available to play anything from Boy George to Beethoven, which sounds like a bloody inconvenient substitute for a radio alarm-clock. The wonderfully ingenuous article, from 1984, is clearly from a land where the phrase 'How much does this thing cost, then?' counted as treason. You could have handed out copies on the miners' picket lines and had a proper revolution going within minutes.

knew, but for most of the crew, sailing her was still not far removed from the hardships of rounding Cape Horn in an old square-rigger.

Britannia was a regular feature of Cowes Week until 1935, under Edward VII and then George V. When George V died she was scuttled in the English Channel. His son Edward VIII was not much interested in keeping her – he spent his only race on board moronically driving golf balls off her stern and into the Solent. (While doing this he must have been beautifully placed to take the massive, low-set boom in the back of the head with great force during a gybe, which would have prevented much subsequent unpleasantness – abdication, fascism, all that.)

Her wheel was preserved, and installed on the next *Britannia*, which in the more enlightened spirit of the modern age wasn't scuttled on retirement, but parked in an Edinburgh suburb as a tourist attraction.

Cowes's royal connections go much further back than that, to George IV in his Prince Regent days. With apologies to anyone with a more sophisticated under-standing of British history than me, that's the berk played by Hugh Laurie in *Blackadder the Third*. He had a talent for dissolute living that would have made him a natural for sailing. Except for one minor detail: he weighed 17 stone, and had a 50-inch waist on his corset. (That's after it's strapped in, remarkably.) It's hard to see what useful function he could have discharged on a yacht apart from ballast, or, at a stretch, a cannonball.

I learned all this stuff off by heart, from a book some-one gave me on the history of yachting or, in my world, all the history that mattered. This apparently completely random, sometimes achingly detailed knowledge used to be a source of some mystification to my history teacher, who couldn't understand how I could come to know George IV's dates, hobbies, debts (extent of) and corset size (extent of), but remain hazy on exactly who Oliver Cromwell was. At least I had the sense not to admit it would have been different if he'd had a yacht.

Oddly, most of what I knew about Cowes Week was historical. I knew about the J-class races in the 1930s, I knew about the origins of the America's Cup in 1851. I knew the first Cowes regatta was in 1826, and that the first edition of the classic Fastnet Race in 1926 had been won by a boat called the *Jolie Brise*, proving that we can't blame the Americans exclusively for the allegedly amusing misspelling of names.

All the remotely recent detail I knew about Cowes Week came from Edward Heath's sailing autobiography, which had some stuff about the 1970s events. (Still before my time.) This was another twisted history, where Heath was a sailor first, and a politician second. Heath may even have felt the same, since he produced his sailing autobiography promptly, and his political memoirs never at all. I felt a considerable sense of betrayal at finding out he hadn't been as good at being Prime Minister as he had been at yacht-racing.[22]

History was all I had, because for some reason the yachting magazines didn't really do Cowes Week in the

[22] In the 1980s Heath even turned up on *Swap Shop*, or perhaps it was *Saturday Superstore*, presumably because there was some respect in which it was going to piss off Margaret Thatcher. His competition question was: 'How many crew are there on my yacht *Morning Cloud*?' I don't know how this can be possible, but I didn't know. I still feel a bit ashamed of that today.

detail you might have expected. There was the photo of Prince Philip, obviously, and there was advice aimed at competitors – what pubs, what restaurants, where the parties were – but not much about the results, or many pictures. There was a strange contradiction; Cowes Week was the most famous and longest-running regatta in the world, part of the Season and just about the only yachting event any non-yachtie had heard of, yet the racing got about the same amount of coverage as the Mirror dinghy national champs.

I'd decided that, cash flow notwithstanding, I couldn't skip Cowes. If need be I could sleep on floors, and live off chips and water for a week. But there were a few problems. I'd originally been planning on going with *Blaze of Glory*, but following damage to the boat in a collision, they skipped the event to get the boat ready for the subsequent offshore race to La Rochelle.

That was OK – Dougal had asked me to sail on *Afterglow*. But most of his crew had used up their holiday and their cash at Cork, so that ride also seemed in doubt. There weren't any boats looking for crew on the internet. I made a few phone calls, sent a few emails, and felt like I was drowning in apathy. I even tried the Cowes Week press office, who asked me what publication I worked for, and didn't stretch themselves to being polite when I admitted it was *Cycling Weekly*. I could kind of see their point.

It began to look very much as if, despite my having counted on it all year, Cowes Week was going to get away from me. A thousand boats expected, four times bigger than any regatta I'd ever been at, and I didn't seem to be able to get involved with any of them. Given the minimal levels of enthusiasm I was encountering, I was curious to know where the 7,000 people I reckoned it was going to take to sail them were going to come from.

My only real hope was Dougal. He still wanted to do Cowes, despite the lack of interest from his crew. After a fortnight of working on it, he finally managed to cobble together a gang of friends of friends, internet crew-search strangers, and essentially anyone who was passing.

The depth of desperation was clear when I received an email that said, 'Michael, can you navigate?' The simple answer to this was, 'No.' Not on water anyway. A few years ago the legendary Eric 'Captain Calamity' Abbott spent a summer being repeatedly rescued from the Irish Sea, sometimes more than once a day, as he attempted to get from Dublin to Holyhead armed only with a three-year-old AA road atlas of the British Isles and a ruler. That was about my level.

'Not really,' I emailed back.

'Anyone can navigate,' came the reply. So that was it settled. I'd been promoted again – way, way beyond my level of competence. Never mind wrecking our racing chances by making bad tactical calls, I was now going to be in a position to kill people. I felt that I was really getting somewhere with my second sailing career. How badly wrong could it go?

Just a few days later I was sitting at the chart table, I was up to about mid-calf level in water – the leaky deck fittings that we didn't manage to fix in Cork – with my ear pressed against the VHF radio, trying to hear the announcement of the course. This was a long list of two-digit numbers designating the marks, and an instruction to leave them to port or starboard. Through the radio, it sounded like a secret code being read into a defective microphone by a man in a tin-roofed shed during a hailstorm.

'Three-sev . . . arboard . . . ero-four . . . ven-zero, por . . .'

This went on for some time. Up on deck were nine people, most of whom I'd never met before that morning, cheerfully assuming that down below their navigator was working out where they were all going for the day. I had to guess about half of it. That didn't matter very much, because when I came to reconcile the numbers with a list of mark names, I couldn't read my writing and had to guess again. The boat bounced off a wave, and the water slopped over the top of my boots.

Of course, they only read out the course ten minutes before the start. Any earlier than that and it would make life too simple. So as the guys upstairs prepared for the off, every few moments a head would pop through the hatch and, with levels of politeness that diminished in proportion to the time left until the gun, enquire where we were supposed to be going. I, meanwhile, tried to grapple with some unfamiliar navigation software (unfamiliar to the extent that until fifteen minutes earlier I'd never seen any navigation software of any description). Dougal had assured me that it was perfectly intuitive, a reassurance that would have been worth more coming from someone who wasn't a former employee of Microsoft.

I found that whatever I did, I could only programme one mark into it. My first attempt at inputting the course resulted in the same mark rounded to port eleven times in succession. The second, and bear in mind I was doing this while being shaken up and down, resulted in the computer crashing. 'Do you,' it said, 'wish to report the error to Microsoft?' I went one better and told Dougal directly. He told me to stop fucking about and give him a course to the first mark.

Navigation is a desk job. The desk shakes, and the seat tries to throw you off, but you still grow weary waiting for the little hour-glass symbol to disappear, and you still, in moments of stress, have to restart the laptop to make it work. It's not a job that has a lot to do with sailing. There are stories about navigators in years gone by who didn't own a set of oilskins, and did their yachting wearing carpet slippers. Clearly they did this on boats that leaked less than *Afterglow*. As water slopped into my boots again, it struck me that if we were sinking it would look just like this.

The other thing about navigation is that in waters like the Solent, it's rather important. Seawater does not just sit there. It's almost always flowing in one direction or another as the tide rises and falls. Unlike Cork, where the tide flows fairly uniformly across the race course, in the Solent it varies dramatically from place to place. It's essential to use this to your advantage. It doesn't matter how brilliantly you sail, if you're heading straight into a 3-knot tide, you're going to get left for dead by anyone smart enough to sail closer inshore and find a 1-knot tide. No one can make a crew look like chumps like the navigator. As I was about to prove.

Once upon a time, sailing Mirrors at Carrickfergus say, you worked this whole tide thing out by knowing when high water was and guessing the rest. Old local hands usually had some more specific knowledge, which was usually wrong. In contrast, aboard *Afterglow*, the laptop had a pretty picture of the Solent, covered in lots of arrows indicating the direction and speed of the tide. Big arrows for fast tide, small arrows for slow. There was a little green boat in the middle of the screen, so I could see exactly where we were. Anyone could work it out, I thought.

The first mark was west of the start. There was a big fat arrow pointing straight from the start towards the first mark. Three knots of tide. Super.

'Dougal,' I said, 'the best bet is to go down the middle and just go with the windshifts.'

I stayed at the chart table, and finished entering the course, then marked it up on a laminated chart so I had an overall view. When I went on deck, a few minutes after the start, I noticed almost all the other boats were crowding together, sailing up the Isle of Wight shore. I thought that was a bit funny, ducked below and checked the laptop, with its reassuring arrow.

Most rookie navigators finding themselves in a minority of one would worry. And, give me some credit, I worried. But I was sure I was right. The big red arrow couldn't lie. The only problem was that as time went on it became clear that the boats tacking as close as they dared by the shoreline were getting to where we were going faster. I worried some more. On the laptop the arrow was still there. It was reality that was wrong.

I'd screwed up. Of course I'd screwed up. I'd screwed up before the race had even begun. What it took me a whole leg to work out was that when I'd restarted the laptop, it had reset the time the software used to calculate tides. My tidal analysis was, indeed, perfect. It was just that it was six-and-a-half hours out of whack. I could not, in the most technical sense possible, have been more wrong. By the time we had struggled against 3 knots of tide to the first mark, our race had been over for quite a while. There was just another five hours of chasing pointlessly round the Solent with an idiot instead of a navigator to go.

The format of the Cowes Week racing had taken me by surprise. I'd expected it to work much like the other major regattas – a variety of races, but with a focus on short, competitive races round specially laid courses, and probably two or three of them a day. Instead, what we got was a long, zigzagging course out into the western Solent past Yarmouth. Then it turned round and zigzagged back, rounding a mark near the island shore, then a mark near the mainland, then back across. The marks were permanent buoys, in fixed locations, which the race officers picked out each morning.

Even allowing for where I'd left us in the race – and everyone seemed very understanding about it: they settled for not speaking to me rather than holding me under water until I stopped struggling – it was not exciting. The length of the race, and the way that the boats were spread out over considerable bits of the Solent, meant that the boat–on–boat racing felt diluted. After the trading-blows-style racing of Cork, I could see why most of my sailing acquaintances had been so lukewarm about Cowes.

It looked wonderful though. A thousand boats is a lot, and it wasn't like Cork, or Tarbert, where most of the boats were quite similar. Cowes featured such rare flowers as *Maximus*, at 100 feet one of the world's biggest racing-yachts. *ABN-Amro* was there, fresh from winning the Round-the-World race, on a publicity junket that casually netted them victory in the week's most prestigious class.

Ellen MacArthur had brought her trimaran *B&Q*, though she wasn't racing. She spent most of the time bobbing around within range of the cameras on Cowes Esplanade. I hadn't realised that her boat was only called *B&Q* on one side – starboard. The port side was a completely different livery, in blue, and the boat was called *Castorama*, for the benefit of any of Ellen's French fans who were dithering about where to buy their Rawlplugs. All the pictures used in the UK media were taken from the orange side. Good trick. I couldn't decide whether *B&Q* looked terrifyingly large for solo sailing – it seemed to cover an area of about an acre – or horribly small for going round the world.

The highlight of our day was coming in towards the finish at Cowes, and racing past the beach at Egypt Point. The pebble beach slopes very steeply, so you can sail just yards off the shore, under what you fondly imagine to be the admiring gaze of holidaymakers and sailing junkies. It's the closest thing sailing has to a grandstand.

Any spectators with radios could pick up live commentary on Cowes FM, which focused particularly on ensuring that no one could mess up without due attention being drawn to it. One boat near us was on the verge of broaching most of the way past the point: 'He's going, he's going, he's . . . he's . . . gone!' The boat kicked its keel in the air, the crew hung on, and a beach full of strangers looked up from their paperbacks to cheer lustily at their misfortune.

It didn't take me longer than the first race to figure out the quality of the racing was not really the point. Five hours to finally understand why the emphasis of all that coverage years ago had been on where to get good chips, not on who won what.

It's an occasion. It's not so much the national athletics championships as the London Marathon going to the seaside to get pissed and try to shag the Royal Meeting at Ascot. It looks great. It sounds great. Cowes has the kind of buzz that only really comes when a whole town gets taken over by one event. You can assume everyone is a sailor, because if they're not, they rent out their house and go somewhere else for the week. If the going rates for the week's rental are anything to go by, the somewhere else is probably a suite at the Dorchester.

Since Cowes is as famous for parties as for sailing, I felt it was important that I sampled the social scene. Months earlier, when *Blaze of Glory* had still been heading for Cowes Week, I'd agreed to buy a ticket to the Royal Corinthian Yacht Club's cocktail party. I'd signed up to this before I asked how much it was going to cost. There was nothing Corinthian about the pricing policy. I was separated from several of my favourite twenty-pound notes with a practised ease.

My going to this party caused some resentment on *Afterglow*. Not that anyone wanted to come with me, but they felt that my navigation had wasted valuable drinking time, and wanted to park the boat and try to catch up. They didn't want to waste yet more time motoring into Cowes to drop me off at a party. The resentment in no way diminished when I came on deck in a blazer and white trousers. I looked like I'd beamed in from 1935.

In the weight-obsessed world of sailing, it had been a bit cheeky to secretly stash my outfit below a bunk cushion. When Dougal pointed this out, I didn't help matters by replying that with a navigator as appalling as me, an illicit blazer was the least of his problems. He refused to leave me ashore, but insisted I get a water taxi instead. He might have been keen to get to the pub, but he hated my spotless shoes and white trousers enough to devote quite some time to hunting down one that had six inches of water in the bottom and seagull crap on all the seats.

At the party, I found my mortgage-sized investment entitled me to drink tepid champagne and eat improbably hot cocktail sausages while admiring the immaculate tailoring of my well-heeled elders and betters.

I ought to admit at this point that this was the first time that I'd ever attended a sailing function that had a dress code. Any kind of dress code. The more standard kind of event is a barbecue where the food is hard to distinguish from the fuel. The greatest formality I'd previously encountered involved rummaging through my kit to find a pair of underpants that had not already been rejected as too revolting to wear on more than, say, two occasions. (Otherwise known as 'smart casual'.)

Nonetheless, the RCYC bash was just what I suspect many people would expect of an après-sail event. And to give the club its due, the champagne may have been tepid, but it was available in unlimited quantities. When one of the guests snatched a bottle off a tray and necked it in one go, the teenaged waiter went to fetch him another one.

It didn't take long to work out what should have been obvious to me: this party was exactly the same as a barbecue – different food, different clothes, and that was it. The conversations were the same: 'He came in high on the mark and over the top of us . . .' 'We were coming across on starboard . . .' The physical nature of sailing bleeds into the conversations; in every gathering of yachties, chat is accompanied by gestures made with an on-edge hand, usually tilted a few degrees off vertical to illustrate whether the hand is on port or starboard tack.

There was a whole roomful of people doing this – over there, by the look of it, was someone whose crew had failed to ease the mainsheet in a gust, causing them to spin out of control and into another boat. And there was someone who'd been caught out at a start and, judging by the extravagance of the karate gestures, had sustained several thousand pounds' worth of damage to his boat.

I drifted around the room on my own – I didn't know very many people, and most of them were deep in conversation and gesture. (I could see one of the *Blaze of Glory* crew describe the occasion a few weeks before where I'd been hit on the head by a spinnaker pole. He seemed to think it was a lot funnier now than he had when I'd been gushing blood all over his shoes.) I drank champagne until I felt slightly fuzzy, which helped me fall into conversations, almost invariably with people who worked in areas of finance I couldn't understand. They'd have been equally perplexed to meet a racing cyclist, but none of them ever really asked. I didn't feel like I was quite there.

Eventually I met a distinguished-looking man, who immediately mistook me for someone else: 'Hello! I didn't expect to see you here! How's Mary? And the family? You off the leash for a few days, eh? We must get you more champagne.'

HELLO SAILOR

I had a volcanically hot sausage in my mouth, and
couldn't put him right. By the time I could have, he was
halfway through a story about having driven the old
Bentley to the south of Spain to pick up some furniture,
only to realise the old Bentley wouldn't be big enough,
'So I had to get a couple of the chaps to follow me down
in the van. Came in damned handy when the gearbox
broke near Toulouse. Chap drove me back in the van,
and left the other chap with the car. Took him bloody
days to get it sorted out.'

My natural sympathy was with the chap abandoned in
Toulouse with a broken antique Bentley, and no
knowledge of the French for 'gearbox'. I fitted in here
not at all, not really.

I left quietly, changed out of my blazer in the public loo
at the Red Jet ferry terminal (I met three other men doing
the same thing) and went to see what else I could find.

There was a big compound near the marina, with a
band, bars, and lots of relaxed-looked people sinking
pints and doing sailing-karate. The bouncer wouldn't let
me in. Apparently I had the wrong kind of competitor's
pass. The properly posh function hadn't been my thing,
and now I couldn't even get into this one. I pressed on to
see what else there was. The pubs on the high street were
packed, and the road was full of people holding drinks.

A crew, in matching sailing-jackets, walked by in the
opposite direction with purpose. 'Hey, Michael,' said one
of them. I thought it was another 'How's Mary' moment,
but it was one of the guys who I'd sailed with in Tarbert,
down with a crew from the Clyde. They took me to the
other end of the town, upriver, where there was another
compound, one that ordinary yachties like us could get

into. I had the feeling that there were three social rungs in Cowes, and I'd spent the evening so far sliding to my natural home: on the bottommost.

I had a beer with my Tarbert friend, then went to find the *Afterglow* lot. While I was looking, I ran into someone I'd met in a pub in Cork, and we agreed I must come sailing with them in the Autumn Series.

This was more like it. I had that sense of belonging that comes only from meeting friends in a crowd. I was beginning to fit in.

For almost everyone who sails, the social element is important, perhaps even essential. In Tarbert, for instance, I had met a cheerful drunkard who explained that he simply hated sailing: 'I only do it because my mates do it. I'm bloody terrified. The best bit of the day is when we tie the damn boat up and hit the beer.'

Every crew that has ever existed feels that it is uniquely gifted in its ability to have a good time. Most of them feel this ability is so striking that everyone else at a regatta will recognise it, and they fancy themselves to be notorious. This is almost always wrong.

But I did once sail with such an outfit. A noisy, boisterous crew of hardcore drinkers and womanisers; men who got into fights, screwed anything that even looked female with no reference whatsoever to the possible consequences, and drank themselves unconscious, sometimes more than once in a day. One of them managed it three times. It was like going sailing with the Hell's Angels.

My last ever sailing had been with these guys. It was a regatta at Bangor, County Down. It was local, but it counted as an away fixture – i.e., you could drink as much as you liked, and shag anything that couldn't run faster than you. Unfortunately for me, my father was at the same event, so I couldn't drink half as much as I'd have liked to, and despite this sobriety meaning I could run faster than anything in a twenty-mile radius, I couldn't shag anything either.

They were mostly a fair bit older than me, in their twenties and thirties, and were not really natural friends for a timid, bookish teenager. Most of the time I was terrified of them. They weren't keen on me either, for the most part, but for one reason and another they were stuck with me. What spoiled a nice, normal, dysfunctional relationship was that despite the fact I didn't like them very much, I wanted to be just like them. I wanted to intimidate women, regularly wake up unsure of where I was, and catch the kinds of diseases that had genitourinary-clinic staff flattening themselves against walls and hitting the panic button.

My father had considerable enthusiasm for these guys and their full-throttle approach to life; I suspect he had a history that was not totally dissimilar, or, at any rate, a history he fancied was quite similar. But he used to give out the most fabulously mixed signals – he would push me out the door to go and have fun with these guys, making it very clear that drinking, swearing, shouting, singing obscene songs and especially, again, drinking, were not going to be tolerated.

The Hell's Angels took shameless advantage of this – there was nothing I couldn't be persuaded to do with a threat to 'tell your dad you've been …' It was no idle threat – one of them, a man in his thirties who behaved like a twelve-year-old snitch, used to do just that. He once went through my kit bag, presumably looking for money, and instead found a condom – a wildly optimistic bit of packing on my part. He gave it to Dad, which was more than a bit embarrassing for both of us.

I put up with this because I had a happy confidence that I'd grow up to be one of the guys. I'm not sure how I thought this was going to happen, or why I was so keen to be part of a gang I didn't really like. Of course, the transformation never happened. It was never going to.

I didn't realise this until I was about eighteen. I should have worked it out a couple of years earlier when Patrick came to Cork Week, the same age as me, and was immediately one of the lads. They recognised him as one of their own instantly, and so did I.

My lack of self-knowledge was breathtaking. It probably still is, but obviously I wouldn't know. At the time I just assumed that since it was my first go at a personality I'd got it wrong. I'd got Lisa Simpson instead of Bart. I suppose I hoped that if I drank enough it would all come good in the end.

I fitted in rather better on *Afterglow*. The crew liked a party, yes, but it was also an environment where I could admit several years playing the bass recorder in an Early Music group without being immediately subjected to some form of ritual humiliation. Another member of the crew played the viola, and someone else, when very drunk, confessed to an A level in Latin and competence on the church organ. These were my people. In a Cowes beer tent we worked our way through a series of jugs of rum and Coke (in which I suspect the rum content was negligible – when I drink five pints of rum and Coke I expect to be drunk). To round off the night, we used someone's press card to gatecrash a rubbish nightclub, the kind of place where your feet make a noise like Velcro when you lift them off the floor and where the DJ is so overexcited at not being stuck in his bedroom that he never stops talking long enough to play a whole track uninterrupted. (This particular DJ looked crushed when all his favourite tracks cleared the floor, and positively suicidal when everyone stormed the dance floor the instant he resignedly played 'Summer of '69', to pogo wildly and play air-guitar. Yachties have their faults, but an excessively avant-garde taste in music is not one of them.)

Whatever my expectations might have been, Cowes had turned out to be exactly the same as Cork, and, minus the rain, the same as Tarbert, and the same as any number of other events. I suppose there are only so many ways to combine alcohol, slightly naff music, terrible take-away food, and a whole bunch of people with a shared interest.

The only difference was that, while in Cork or Tarbert this was all there had been, in Cowes you knew that somewhere above you were the rounds of formal cocktail parties and dinners, and the corporate entertainment functions, like Wimbledon or Ascot. That was the complaint I heard repeatedly about Cowes Week: it was 'too corporate'. It was a fantastically ironic instinct towards egalitarianism.

In the meantime, though, the microcosm of the class system kept the ordinary yachties rather meek and reserved. Or maybe it was just that most of them were a lot closer to home, and the exact provisions of the 'stays on tour' rules were rather more fuzzy. Whatever it was, it all felt slightly flat. All the other evenings passed like the first, sitting round a table, drinking the sponsor's complimentary rum and bitching about how corporate sponsors were ruining Cowes.

I almost found myself thinking that the Hell's Angels would have brightened it up a bit. Almost.

After my very shaky beginning I felt I managed to navigate all right; I'd have given myself about seven out of ten. I was right quite a lot more often than I was wrong, and considering I had to work out the complexities of the tidal streams, while trying to keep track of what the wind was doing, that was a reasonable result. I suspected that part of the reason I took to it was because on the monitor I had a plain view of what we were doing – a little boat in the middle of a screen. It looked just like the diagrams in all the books.

That didn't mean I didn't make mistakes. But I managed to cover most of them up, one of the main requirements of a successful navigator. Some mistakes were bigger than others. On the Thursday, for example, I crashed us into the Isle of Wight because I'd forgotten it was there. I'd plotted a straight-line course out in the eastern Solent, and failed to notice that the line was not *exclusively* on the blue bit of the map. I confidently assured Dougal that all was well, and that this was the optimum route, and that he should stop arguing and trust me, while I moved on to assess the much more complicated next leg, across the tide and over to Portsmouth.

I exaggerate when I said crash. It was more of a bump into some mud. In fact, I'd have got away with it if I'd said, 'Well, I was trying to stay inshore, out of the tide, didn't quite get it spot on, sorry.' I gave it away when I bolted out of the main hatch and yelped, 'What the hell was that?'

I even steered the boat for about half a leg one afternoon, when the electronics had gone on the fritz and needed Dougal's silicon fingers to fix them. It was the first time I'd steered in a race since I gave up dinghying, and I fell some way short of brilliant. But with the blue sea and sky I was quite a lot of the way to my childhood dreams. It's just that *Afterglow* was about half the size I'd had in mind, and instead of the crack professional crew I wanted, I had an uncooperative group of hangovers. My first command, a call of 'Ready about!', was greeted with a grumpy, 'Fuck off.' I had to ask three times. Even then, it was clear they were just humouring me. It was just like Mirror sailing all over again.

I didn't really care. Standing in manly fashion behind the wheel I felt like I had recovered another few months of wasted youth. I really could do this. Teenage me might have been, just slightly, impressed.

The problem was I still wanted more. I wanted to race on bigger boats, under warmer skies, and I wanted to win some races, or at least get close enough to the front of the fleet that 'winning' seemed like a relevant concept. I just had no idea how to make this happen. I felt I was good enough to be part of a winning team, but getting onto the team was another matter.

The best I could do was call at an internet-café in Cowes and send another volley of emails, looking for racing in some of the big autumn events in the Mediterranean. I got no responses, presumably because if any of them could have organised that they'd have done it for their own benefit. All I could do was hope that as the events approached, other crew would drop out, and someone would think of me.

In the meantime, I was going to be out of touch for a few days. It was time for a bit of adventure. I'd done a lot of sailing around buoys in inshore waters on short races. That was the side of the sport that I liked best – intense, tactical, fast paced. But now I could feel the need to do something that might constitute an excuse to make tearful to-camcorder speeches about how awful it was.

Luckily this yearning was easy to satisfy. *Blaze of Glory* had been repaired, ready for my longest-standing commitment. The La Rochelle race was the first thing I'd talked to Mike and Helen about, way back at the Chelsea FC party, and I'd been looking forward to it ever since. It was 450 miles, which might take up to a week, since most of it was into the prevailing winds. It sounded just right.

Chapter Nine

Suhaili

EVERYONE KNOWS THAT ABOUT 70 PER CENT OF THE earth is covered in water. Almost no one believes any of it, not really. That's not surprising. If you stand on a beach on a clear day and look out to sea, the horizon is about three miles away. That's all most of us ever see. But for every area of land you can think of – your garden, a tennis court, Belgium – there is more than twice as much water out there somewhere.

If the jet airliner has achieved nothing else, it's erased the oceans from the world's consciousness. When I went to Melbourne for the Commonwealths, apart from the hassles with my luggage – a recurring theme in my life – getting there and back was a piece of cake. Heathrow, aeroplane, Singapore, Melbourne. The only water I saw was in the plastic cup I elbowed into the lap of the man sitting next to me.

But if I'd gone to the Melbourne Olympics fifty years earlier, I'd have seen loads of water and I'd have had something like six weeks to admire it sliding slowly past.

The other thing I'd have noticed was that there was nothing else to notice. Away from regular shipping routes the blue bits are as close to empty as to provoke no arguments. The occasional whale, with its pursuing pack of Japanese whalers and the whalers' pursuing pack of environmentalists, the odd jellyfish on its way home to Belfast Lough for Christmas, and that's about it.

The ocean is just made for racing. All that space. You can go anywhere you like, from any port to any other port, via whatever selection of intermediate points you like. You can race across the Atlantic. By a very happy geographical coincidence, you can race all the way round the world, if that's what you fancy. You can race, downwind the whole way, from Los Angeles across the Pacific to Hawaii, where the local bars will dispatch hula girls with complimentary drinks to greet you on arrival. I can see the appeal.

The problem is that most of these events are really beyond the reach of your average amateur crew. They involve a great deal of time, a fair amount of expense, and, if they're to be done safely, a lot of experience and no small amount of boat upgrades. If it all goes wrong, the one thing you can't do is get out and walk. When it comes down to it, in open ocean, you can float only marginally better than you can fly.

For most of us, the closest we can get to the blue-water adventure-playground are offshore races that remain in essentially coastal waters. Out of sight of land, but not out of reach of rescue. The Fastnet Race, held in odd-numbered years from Cowes to the south-west corner of Ireland and back to Plymouth, is the most famous. It's probably best known for the tragic 1979 edition where fifteen competitors lost their lives after an unforecasted storm struck the fleet, much of which was not as well prepared or equipped as it might have been.[23]

In non-Fastnet years, the organisers offer a different long offshore event. The Cowes–La Rochelle race was what had come out of the bag this time round. A whiff of adventure.

In best Captain Cook fashion, I spied out the route on a globe. That turned out to be a mistake, since it made the voyage of 450 miles look like a trip to the paper shop. From a blue smear above the Isle of Wight that looked like a printing error, round the top corner of France at Ushant, across the Bay of Biscay, and into La Rochelle. The whole affair would be comfortably contained within an area the size of my little fingernail. Even allowing for the fact it was a rather small globe, that seemed a bit pathetic.

It was the Sunday after Cowes Week, and evening was already falling over the Solent when the starting-gun fired. With up to six days of racing ahead of us, the first thing we did was muff up the start. Naturally we were over the line before the gun went, and had to go back afterwards to re-cross it. That put a certain strain on things from the beginning.

[23] When I was doing some research for this book, I re-read John Rousmaniere's *Fastnet Force Ten*, which was the source of the priceless advice that you should only abandon ship and get into a life raft if boarding the raft involves a step up, rather than down. It's an absolute last resort. A raft is, at its heart, a small bouncy-castle. In 1979 many of them fell apart, while the boat the crew had left stayed afloat. Rafts are supposedly much better now, but the handful of people I know who've ever been in one were still rather underwhelmed by the experience.

There were only eight of us on board *Blaze of Glory*. That was probably two fewer than we should have had, but it still allowed plenty of latitude for a highly vertical management structure. The senior executives were Mike, skipper and my watch leader, Mac, the owner, and David, leader of the other watch. Bryan, the navigator, was a sort of management consultant – as I'd found navigating on *Afterglow*, it's a job that's not quite about sailing.

Then there was twenty-something Alex, who didn't have a seat on the board quite yet, but would soon. And below him, on the works floor, were his younger brother C.J., Karen and me. All three of us thought we were the senior shop-steward. It didn't matter, because it turned out *Blaze of Glory* was a non-unionised boat.

I was unpopular the instant the gun fired, because I was given the blame for being over the line. Someone had to take the rap, and the general consensus was that it might as well be me.

Within thirty minutes or so, as we beat out of the Solent in the face of a building south-westerly, Mike decided it was time to change down to a small headsail. What had been a warm evening had become cold and windy, but a request for two minutes to put on foul-weather jackets was denied. C.J. and I got drenched doing that change; it was to be days before my mid-layers dried out. We muttered furiously to each other.

It turned into a very dark night. We made another five sail changes in the next two hours, from the code 3 to the 2, to the 3, the 2, the 1 and the 2. Each time the new sail was hauled forward to the bow and hoisted, and the old one pulled down, then folded carefully into its bag. Doing all this on a sloping, wet, windy deck is reasonably difficult, and it's no easier in the dark. You got sweaty doing the change, then froze when you went back to the rail. It was a relief when the next change came, because it was the only way to get warm.

At 1 a.m., David and his watch – Karen and Alex – went below. Mac and Bryan went too – neither was in a watch, but they were on-call to help with manoeuvres three crew couldn't do on their own. On deck, Mike steered, I trimmed the sails by torchlight, and C.J. sat on the rail, probably two-thirds asleep and, I'd guess, so cold he was beginning to hallucinate.

A small boat at sea is a strange mix of agoraphobia and claustrophobia. So much space, clear to the horizon, and a world that ends at the perimeter of the deck. On a dark night all you can see are a few feet of threatening, black water round your haven, maybe some phosphorescence in the wake, and beyond that an infinity of impenetrable nothing. The lifelines round the deck seem very low and very fragile. If you're of an imaginative disposition it's rather creepy.

But at least sailing at night makes you a better sailor, because it removes the distractions and makes you concentrate. On dinghy training-weekends, we used to try helming with closed eyes, to learn to sense the wind and waves through the helm and the sheets. I admit that I never actually did this without peeking, because it involved having faith that your crew would tell you if you were going to hit something. If I was going to trust Dobbs I might as well have sailed into the harbour wall with my eyes open and got it over with.

Shortly before 4 a.m., C.J. boiled the kettle, made three cups of tea, and woke David's watch. After a five-minute hand-over period, Mike, C.J. and I got into the still-warm bunks. And that was the pattern established. Three hours on, three hours off. For however long it took.

Down below, in a double bunk that would have been a bit too cosy even if sleeping with C.J. had been high on my list of life-ambitions, we tried to get to sleep. I kept having strange, half-conscious dreams prompted by the sound of water bubbling past just inches away on the other side of the hull. It was like trying to sleep in a cistern. But it was nice to get out of the cold.

At least it was until the guys upstairs decided to tack. That put me on the downhill side of the bunk, and all eighteen slumbering stones of C.J. rolled across it like a log and settled comfortably on top of me. C.J. was not experiencing any detectable difficulty sleeping. I'd have kicked him, but I didn't have enough room for a back-swing, and biting him seemed excessively unfriendly. I was only rescued at 7 a.m. when Karen appeared with a cup of tea and demanded our presence on deck. I'd asked for coffee, but I wasn't inclined to be picky.

The wind had become light, and fog had arrived. The colour of the sea and the sky matched perfectly, and a fine drizzle didn't so much fall as just hang in the air, quietly saturating everything it touched. I thought of a word for it: frizzle. But no one was interested. There was no horizon, and everything had a uniform, faintly brown tinge, like old Tupperware. Mike was steering exclusively on the compass bearing because there was absolutely nothing to point the boat at. Up, down, left, right, it was all the same. Glassy swells rolled out of nowhere, rocked the boat and knocked over your tea, and rolled away again.

I have to admit that there wasn't a lot of adventure going on. It felt a lot more like boredom. You couldn't even revel in being out of sight of land, because we may as well have been in the middle of a decent-sized swimming pool for all we could see to the contrary. No running, no dive-bombing, no petting. I laughed at the thought of it, then had to explain what I was laughing at. It went down every bit as well as the 'frizzle' comment.

'I think perhaps you should concentrate on the sails,' said Mike.

The sails were hanging like wet washing. I concentrated on them like mad.

Whatever edge the proceeding had ever possessed finally vanished with the arrival of the day's only repast: a rather incongruous Marks & Spencer vegetarian ready-meal. Excitement, adventure and really wild mushroom lasagne. It wasn't something I'd normally have been very enthusiastic about. I ate it straight from the hot foil-dish like an over-excited Labrador.

A lot of the long offshore racing was new to me, because I didn't do much of it when I was growing up. There was an offshore series out of Belfast Lough, but the races were rarely more than twenty-four hours long, and I didn't get to do very many of those because they usually clashed with the exam season or some allegedly indispensable geography field-trip. Because these races were shorter, crews didn't usually take watches – you just tried to stay awake for twenty-four hours, and you were a wuss if you couldn't do it.

I didn't really feel I was missing out. At the time I wanted to be a star at the shorter, inshore round-the-buoys events, things like the Olympics or the America's Cup. In motor-racing terms I wanted to be a Formula 1 star, not a rally driver. The longer races just seemed cold, wet and tedious, and frankly I could get all that on the field-trip and get a geography A level in the deal for free.

It was an unusual piece of contrarianism from me. The 70s and 80s came hard on the heels of the late 1960s and a mania for offshore adventuring, especially single-handed. Sir Francis Chichester, Robin Knox-Johnston, Clare Francis, Chay Blyth, the first Round-the-World race – men and women vanished over the horizon and came back months later with hair-raising tales of adventure, which was a bit of luck since the boat had normally been paid for with a book advance.[24]

Of all these books and all these heroes, for me one stood out. Robin Knox-Johnston was the first to sail non-stop, single-handed round the world. NASA were knocking together the first Apollo missions in 1968 when Knox-Johnston and a year's supply of corned beef set out from Falmouth in a 32-foot wooden boat called *Suhaili* that looked like an antique even at the time. He plodded round the world at an average speed that was little more than a brisk walk, and came back ten months later, wild-looking, bearded, and wearing filthy oilskins, having been out of radio contact for the previous eight and a half months. Prior to a sighting off the Azores a fortnight earlier, there had been no trace of him since he passed New Zealand. I wouldn't say he'd been given up for dead, but I don't think anyone was renewing his magazine subscriptions.

---

[24] Either book advances were much bigger in those days or boats were a great deal cheaper.

Thirteen weeks later the crew of *Apollo 11* sat themselves on top of a huge bomb and were blasted to the moon, with live TV coverage, a working radio and wearing the coolest item of clothing ever invented, the spacesuit. From the vantage point of the early 1980s, it was hard to believe these events had happened so close together. In those few weeks, one era had finished and another had begun.

I was the only child in a thousand miles who would rather have met Robin Knox-Johnston than Neil Armstrong. His was a heroism I could understand – I felt sharply the fear he described in *A World of my Own* when, seeing a huge wave rearing up behind him in the depths of the ferocious Southern Ocean, he realised it was probably going to swamp *Suhaili*, and quite certainly sweep him off the deck. I could summon that scene in detail. Knox-Johnston saved himself by scurrying up the rigging to avoid the rogue wave as it broke over the deck. I could imagine him clinging to a mast that seemed to emerge directly from an angry ocean, with no boat to be seen. If I closed my eyes I thought I could feel what it would be like.

Eventually *Suhaili* broke the boiling surface of the sea. She could just as easily have not, and Knox-Johnston would have vanished without trace. No one would have known what happened, or where, or when. I used to lie awake at night, scaring myself to the point of tears by imagining what it would be like to find myself swimming alone in the freezing Southern Ocean. I could not decide whether it would be worse to have the boat sink from under me, or to fall overboard and watch her sailing away as I tried to stay afloat 1,000 miles from land. The definitive last word in dying alone.

On the other hand, one of the most life-affirming things I've ever read was the last few pages of the book, through the western approaches, and into the Channel – the very waters of the La Rochelle race. The very best kind of lap of honour, where you're still technically competing, but you've all but won already. You can enjoy the sensation of triumph to the full. I was moved on each of the hundreds of times I read it by the exchange as he sailed into Falmouth, and the customs officers in their launch came alongside and asked, knowingly, the customary question: 'Where from?'

'Falmouth,' replied Knox-Johnston. Never has Falmouth seemed more romantic, though that might, of course, just be me.

Knox-Johnston was the only competitor of nine to reach the finish in one of the oddest races ever seen, the *Sunday Times* Golden Globe, for the first and fastest non-stop solo circumnavigations. You could set off when you liked over the summer of 1968. There were prizes for both first home and fastest elapsed time. Knox-Johnston started early, in probably the slowest boat, and no one much fancied his chances. But over the next few months the others variously gave up, sank, concluded they didn't like sailing after all, decided that they'd rather go to Tahiti, or realised they were the second coming. Like I say, it was an odd race.

Chay Blyth, for example, started the race without knowing how to sail. On departure he got a friend to sail out of the harbour first so that he'd be able to copy him. He later described frantically leafing through a how-to-sail manual during a gale as 'Hell with instructions'. Unfortunately, by the time he reached South Africa, his boat was falling apart. It was clear even to a non-sailor that entering the Southern Ocean would be suicidal, so he quit.[25]

At the other end of the experience scale was Bernard Moitessier. From the outset, he looked like a good bet for the win. But somewhere in the South Atlantic, at a point where Knox-Johnston was all but waiting for him to surf past on the next big wave, Moitessier decided that victory would involve money, fame and media exposure, and concluded that he'd rather just sail on round the world again. He said it was 'to save my soul'. Hence Tahiti.

The whole race, however, was overshadowed by the tragedy of Donald Crowhurst. He staked everything on winning – his house, his business and his family's financial future. And gradually his preparations turned to farce. The boat was late being launched. Relentless media demands started to act as a distraction. A delivery trip from the builders in Norfolk to his departure port of Teignmouth that should have taken a few days took a fortnight.

The hours before he set sail, late in the afternoon of the last day allowed by the rules, were chaotic. Almost all the spares he might need were left behind. Even when he finally left, he got his halyards tangled, and had to be towed to shore to sort them out and try again.

I have a certain perspective on this. A few years ago I made an attempt on a cycling world record. Very gradually, everything went wrong. The bike I'd had built was late, and when it arrived it wasn't of the required

---

[25] Lest there be any slur on Blyth's hard-as-nails credentials, he later became the first man to sail single-handed round the world the wrong way – west about, against the prevailing winds and currents. This is a spectacularly hard-core thing to do.

specification. I got distracted by logistics, didn't look for help early enough, and ended up doing administration when I should have been doing cycling. If it had all fallen apart at once, I'd have upped and quit, but the bricks dropped out of the wall one by one.

Comparisons with childhood heroes were not the first thing I thought about as the chaos mounted, but it doesn't take a genius to spot that I had more in common with Crowhurst than with Knox-Johnston. Except that for me failure would only be failure. For Crowhurst, failure would most probably mean a lonely death. The night before he left, his wife reported that he cried for hours. He knew what the attempt would mean, but he couldn't stop it happening.

The result is well known – in a desperate attempt to save his life, he sailed aimlessly around in the South Atlantic, waiting for the rest of the competitors to round Cape Horn and head home. Then he'd slip back into the race. The idea wasn't to win, but to perform respectably, and hope that that was enough to keep his sponsors on side. Winning would have meant a detailed examination of his logbooks, and guaranteed detection of the fraud.

He killed time making audiotapes and films. He faked a log for a whole circumnavigation, complete with reverse-calculated sextant sightings, a mathematical feat of considerable difficulty, and radioed fake positions, in the vaguest possible terms.

It all went wrong when, firstly, Moitessier went to Tahiti, and then the boat of the last other competitor, Nigel Tetley, sank when he was just a couple of weeks from home. Suddenly Crowhurst was going to win the race for fastest time. He would be disgraced.

He lost his mind. His real logbook charted a descent into full gothic lunacy, with the conviction he was a divine being, and an obsession with time. When his boat was found by a passing ship, there was no sign of Crowhurst. It's assumed that in his madness he jumped overboard. It's the only thing I can think of that would be worse than being swept away in a storm.[26]

All this rather destructive enthusiasm for sailing round the world had been started by Francis Chichester. An adventurer of a high order, he'd been the first man to fly from New Zealand to Australia, and the second man to fly from Britain to Australia. He was the first to sail solo round the world with only one stop, in Australia. His arrival back in the UK was watched by millions on live TV, and he was subsequently knighted by the Queen at Greenwich in a deliberate echo of Elizabeth I and Francis Drake. She presumably muttered something about restoring pride to a great seafaring nation, or some such pre-moon landing sentiment.

Chichester also wrote a book. It was, essentially, one very long whinge. The weather was bad. He didn't feel well. He complained frequently and at length about his boat, which he felt had been very badly designed. He kept having to get out of his bunk and fix problems. (Invariably referred to as 'shemozzles', a word I was hard

---

[26] See Peter Nichol's *A Voyage for Madmen* for a terrific account of the Golden Globe. On Crowhurst specifically, see *The Strange Last Voyage of Donald Crowhurst* by Nicholas Tomalin and Ron Hall, one of the most horribly compelling books ever written about sailing. The transcripts of Crowhurst's last log entries make for exceptionally uncomfortable reading. Knox-Johnston announced he would donate his prize to Crowhurst's family in the few days after the drifting boat was found, when it was assumed he'd simply fallen overboard. He stood by this decision after the full story emerged.

pressed, even at the age of eleven, to believe featured heavily in his internal dialogue. Maybe if you call them fuck-ups, you don't get knighted.) He gave every impression of having simply hated sailing round the world.

Much of my affection for Knox-Johnston (who had to wait another twenty-five years for his knighthood) was that in contrast to Chichester, he clearly quite enjoyed most of the voyage, and retained a considerable sense of humour.

This was despite appearing to be almost as old-bufferish at the age of twenty-nine as Chichester at sixty-six. It was clear that Knox-Johnston was not going to be even a tiny bit upset that the voyage meant he would miss the release of the *White Album* and *Yellow Submarine*. This is relevant because I've always tried to repress the certain knowledge that if I'd lived through the 60s, the Beatles would have been a bunch of badly dressed young men of limited talent, who ought to have made a group appointment at the barber's, and then got proper jobs.[27]

What the La Rochelle race taught me was that if I had Crowhurst's gift for organisation, I had Chichester's talent for whinging. I kept a diary of the trip. (Originally I'd planned to make a video diary, but I realised that being caught doing my best tearful Ellen MacArthur impersonation into a camera might come under the heading of Taking the Piss.) My diary is a dead ringer for Chichester's book.

As early as the first hours of the race: 'Bloody sail

[27] Incidentally, in my mid-teens I made the rather unexpected discovery that my father had been on the production team for one of the Rolling Stones' early TV appearances. 'Wow!' I said, finally impressed. 'What were they like?' After a moment's thought, he said, 'Scruffy.'

change – got soaked. My underpants will be wet all week now. I'm hating this already.'

A little later: 'Had to get out of my bunk to help with a sail change. Bloody unfair.' It wasn't really all that unfair, it was what I was there for.

Twenty-four hours in: 'The new watch was FIVE MINUTES LATE coming on. FIVE FUCKING MINUTES. I suppose they had to fold their pyjamas.'

Thirty-six hours in: 'My coffee had sugar in it. I mean bloody hell, how many times do I have to tell them, how many?!?!'

And: 'I'm sick of ready-meals, I'm sick of soup, I'm sick of muesli bars, I'm sick of "would you like a fun-sized Mars bar?", I'm sick of sailing, I'm sick of sail changes, I'm sick of sail trimming, I'm sick of this boat, I'm sick of everyone on it, I'm sick of this race, I'm sick of the night watches, I'm sick of the day watches, I'm sick of sea and I'm sick of sky.'

These were just the diary's highlights. What's odd is that, overall, I'd say I was having quite a nice time. After the first couple of days, the wind veered towards the north, and instead of the slog to Ushant that we'd been expecting, most of it was fast reaching, often under spinnaker. It was clearly going to be a quick passage, closer to four days than to the six that we'd anticipated.

The thing is that, in such an isolated environment, where there is so little of anything much, where you're perpetually tired, the small things are all there are, and they drive you nuts. MacArthur's much lampooned videos were not tearful because she was on her own, thousands of miles from safety, and doing statistically one of the most dangerous activities there is, they were tearful because the generator was playing up, the instruments were on the blink, or an albatross had crapped in her Pot Noodle.

Karen, for instance, normally made the hot drinks for our watch as we came on. At least half the time mine was a drink with added humour – it was tea rather than coffee, or it had six sugars in it, or it was stone cold. This drove me to distraction, which Karen found hugely entertaining.

The new watch coming on deck late was equally infuriating, especially at night. It seems trivial, and it is trivial, it's just that you're tired, you've been working hard, you're cold, and longing for your sleeping bag and a few minutes of peace. Most of all, you're counting down the minutes until you can put the kettle on for their drinks, make the drinks, wake them up, and finally expect them on deck. Five minutes late is five minutes that you're not in a bunk, *and they are.*

I rarely went to sleep properly. I was always vaguely aware of what was happening; I could hear general activity, movements on deck. I developed the most sensitive antennae for a manoeuvre that might require the help of the off-watch. You tried as hard as you could to pretend it wasn't happening, but you knew you were about to be woken up, and that while it would only be for ten or fifteen minutes, you'd come back down wide awake and not get within hailing distance of being asleep again for the rest of the watch. (This was, perhaps not coincidentally, when most of the infectiously cheerful diary entries were made.)

But, on night three, I was finally sound asleep. I had a warm, fuzzy feeling. Just guess what happened next.

'Mike! Get your ass up here, dude!' It was Alex. 'We're gybing, need you on the point.'

When I'd gone off watch at 10 p.m. it had been a nice evening, moderate breeze, moonlight, easy sea. A couple of hours later it was very dark, very cold, and quite rough.

I went to the bow and braced myself at the base of the forestay. C.J. was at the mast, and beyond him I couldn't see anything other than the white light at the stern reflecting off the waves behind us.

'Ready!' C.J. called back to the cockpit.

'Trip!' came the command.

At this point the U-shaped fitting at the end of the pole was supposed to open, so the pole could drop away from one corner of the spinnaker and swing down to me. I would slot a new rope into the fitting, then let the pole swing back up to the sail's other corner. C.J. pulled the tripping line on the pole and . . . precisely nothing happened.

'Tension on the sheet!' I shouted into the wind. The pole was being wedged fast by the pressure that was still on the rope passing through its end-fitting. If the tension from the sail was taken up on a different rope, that ought to sort it out. C.J. passed it back to the cockpit. There was no response, apart from a distinctly testy shout of, 'Come on, guys, trip!' Nothing. C.J. repeated the request. 'Trip it harder!' was the reply.

A tripping line does not work this way. Either it has been pulled or it has not. With the greatest respect, this bit of advice was precisely the equivalent of ringing a computer support line and having a conversation that goes, 'Hi, my PC won't switch on.'

'Have you pressed the power button?'

'Yes.'

'Have you pressed the power button?'

'Yes.'

'Try pressing it harder.'

The guys at the back resolved the stand-off by carrying on with the gybe regardless. Or, in support-line terms, 'Sir, I'm getting bored with this, so I suggest you hold down the control and alt keys, and hit the delete key as hard as you can with an axe.'

The boom banged across to the new side. The spinnaker collapsed and started to flog madly. Before C.J. or I could do anything about it, it had wrapped itself in a knot round the rigging, far above the foredeck in the night sky.

It was stuck fast, flapping away, and generally mocking us for our incompetence. It took Alex, Bryan, C.J. and me, with much utterly indispensable advice from everyone else, to finally, half an hour later, pull the sail down and untangle it. For a good ten minutes it looked like I was going to have to climb up into the dark with a knife to cut it free. I was profoundly pleased that I did not have to do so.

In the midst of the operation, an exchange took place between Alex and me, the full significance of which only became clear later:

Alex: 'Here, get this out of the way.' He handed me the end of a halyard. The rest of it stretched into the night above us.

Me: 'Is it clear?'

Alex: 'Yes.'

Alex just meant it was clear of the sail; I assumed he meant it was clear of everything, and ready for use. Assumption is, as they say, the mother of all shemozzles. When we packed the kite and re-hoisted it, the halyard was still round the forestay, so we got everything tangled up again. By the time we dropped the sail and unknotted it for a second time, the whole affair had taken three-quarters of an hour. The longest gybe in history.

Sailing being a team sport, where maintaining the morale of the group is an important part of good racing, it was only natural that I got the blame. No one said so, of course, but when Mac complained the following morning that, 'We're sailing like fucking amateurs,' I knew who he meant.

Or later, when Bryan suggested to Mike that it would be a good idea to sail a higher course, then gybe back across, Mike glanced at me, and said, 'No, we can't risk another gybe.'

It was a pity. The morning was beautiful. The sea was blue, and half an hour after dawn the sky was a delicate indigo, deepening towards the zenith into a violet that looked almost solid. I tried to take a photograph of it, but all I got was plain old-fashioned sky. The camera carefully filtered out the poetry.

It was clear that this was going to be our last morning at sea; Bryan gave us an ETA of 4 p.m., and backed it up with lots of technical jargon about 'mark-closing velocities' and 'optimised angles'. And on the approach to La Rochelle, the result began to shake out. One of the frustrations of offshore racing is that you often have very little idea where the opposition is. There had been a closing-up of competitors round Ushant, but even then we'd been rather unsure. Now most of the other boats in our class were in sight. It was apparent that we were not doing well. Each positive ID through the binoculars darkened the mood further.

'If only we hadn't spent an hour fucking about last night,' said Alex. Mike and Mac agreed. I knew they were looking at me, but I kept admiring the sky. At that moment its delicate coloration was not nearly as attractive as the idea of single-handed sailing. The last few hours felt like a long time – the race was over, we'd lost, but we were still stuck out there. The opposite to Knox-Johnston's triumphant final miles.

I'm whinging again. There is obviously something about offshore sailing that brings it out. It wasn't that bad. I was even going to be sorry to stop. Well, very slightly. I could see an appeal to heading south to the equator, maybe a stop in Cape Town. They'd forget about the gybe in a thousand miles. I'd stop sulking in two.

It all felt so very, very far from the rest of life – no email, no phones, no news, and no time to think about any of it anyway. I don't have a particularly hectic life, but it was still nice to leave it behind for a few days. Off Ushant, my phone had picked up a signal and received a few messages; I deleted them without looking, or thinking twice. When we got ashore, on the other hand, I knew I needed to get back to the UK, answer email, make phone calls, write two magazine articles that were overdue even before I left home, use the payments from them to get the roof fixed …

Nearly all the voyagers' books stop dead when the hero yachtsman crosses the finishing line. It's easy to see why. It's the last word in travelling rather than arriving. It wasn't as if La Rochelle was somewhere the crew of *Blaze of Glory* particularly wanted to be. No more than Falmouth was where Knox-Johnston wanted to be. We crossed the line, tidied up, and Mac said, 'Mike, do you think they deserve a beer?' Mike agreed that we did, although he had to think about it. We got a tin of warm Boddingtons each. Even me.

And that was it. We had a meal, a few drinks, and at last a night's sleep. I left early the following morning, went to the airport and bought myself a flight home. As the plane banked over the Bay of Biscay, I looked down at the water. 'Stuff that,' I thought, and read an article in the in-flight magazine about Tahiti. It sounded lovely.

Chapter Ten

132056

DESPITE THE COMPLAINTS SCRIBBLED FURIOUSLY INTO my race diary, the La Rochelle race had been all right. I could remember it being all right. There had been some good sailing; the buzz of charging downwind at night in a breeze, the intensity of crewing a small boat out of sight of land, and some fabulously coloured sunsets and dawns.

But the more I thought about the whole thing, the more my recollection of this perfect-adequacy seemed to crumble away. To summarise: I'd wanted to be Robin Knox-Johnston. Instead, it had been not much more thrilling than eight of us renting a people carrier and driving to La Rochelle, slowly.

I seemed determined, from some stupid, childish lack of perspective, to ignore the obvious fact that I wasn't Robin Knox-Johnston. I didn't give myself any credit for being part of the genuine, if not quite earth-shattering achievement of racing 450 miles, day and night, armed only with the winds and tides, our wits and skills, twenty kilos of M&S ready-meals and a quarter-of-a-million-pounds' worth of boat.

This was exactly the kind of historical revisionism that has, over many years, led an old schoolfriend of mine to the conviction that he had had an unhappy childhood just because it didn't involve secret passages, islands, lighthouses and adventures with enemy spies. He was happy enough at the time – I can remember, and, for that matter, so can he. But he's miserable now.

I didn't really hear from the *Blaze of Glory* team again – I did send an email a day or two after I got back saying thanks, and that I'd enjoyed the sail, but it was trumped a few hours later by one saying, 'An especial thanks to Mac for allowing us the privilege of being allowed to sail his yacht with him …' The only subsequent contact was thirteen months later, when I got a bill for the food. It might not have been quite the sail I wanted, but I got a year's free credit on the lasagne, and you can't complain about that.

It was mid August by the time I got back. Suddenly there was the glint of melancholy that there always is in high summer; a premonition of the coming autumn, the winter, the cold and the wind, and the end of the sailing season. I'm almost embarrassed to admit it, but even in my mid-thirties, there is more than a hint of dreading going back to school.

I'd made progress all year, but really, honestly, I was still a long way from my pro dreams. There had been no trace of my blue-skies, blue-seas, T-shirt-and-shades sailing, or my big glamorous yacht. While I had wanted to make progress, to see how good a sailor I still was, I had wanted all that too. Probably more than I'd realised. Believe me, there wasn't a lot of that kind of thing about on Belfast Lough, and I reckoned I'd waited long enough. But now the summer was almost gone.

I think this is the point where I'm supposed to announce that it was time for desperate measures. Drastic action. Take the thing by the scruff of the neck. But I'm not really a desperate-measures kind of guy. However, I did have an option that was, if not quite dangerous, at least a bit of a gamble.

Back in January, when I'd sent emails to every skipper who had an entry on the RORC register, I'd received a reply (the first one, I think) from someone called Gordon, who gave no second name and no boat name, but said that he was looking for crew for the Swan Cup. He said he needed a bowman, or possibly a mastman, or possibly a headsail trimmer, he wasn't sure. I sent him an email saying I'd be anything he wanted me to be, and got one back saying welcome on board, sailor. And that was about all I heard for months.

To put this in some context, the Swan Cup is an event exclusively for Swan yachts, made in Finland, apparently out of compressed fifty-pound notes. They are designed by the finest designers, built to the very highest standards, awash with finely crafted teak and mahogany, and in just about all respects, everything a sailing yacht (I don't think 'boat' is appropriate here) should be.

Unlike a pure-bred racing-boat, an old Swan is covetable, so, remarkably for something that floats, it has a resale value that's greater than the cost of towing it out to sea and drilling a hole in its bottom.

To create the Swan Cup, you take a hundred or so of

these wonderful yachts, ranging in size from 40 feet to considerably over 100, and you have a regatta for them in Porto Cervo, an exclusive resort founded by the Aga Khan on the lovely, craggy north-east corner of Sardinia. You get it sponsored by Rolex, a company that in this context makes cheap watches, but at least has deep pockets. You hold the event in mid-September, when the heat of the summer has begun to mellow but the sea is still warm and the evenings are balmy. It is tacitly acknowledged that this is not really the zenith of cut-throat competition, so you lay on a lavish social scene of a rather classier aspect than a beer-tent and a sticky-floored disco. The attraction of all this is, I trust, becoming clear.

After my initial contact with Gordon, I mentioned that I was doing the Swan Cup to an old sailing friend of my dad's. He was almost speechless with envy. But of course, as the long silence over the summer went on, I began to wonder if it was really happening. Eventually I sent an email, and got a reply saying, 'Yep, it's on, catch this flight out of Gatwick.' Then, despite my sending a couple of emails carefully tooled to demand a response without looking too needy – 'Hi – just to say I'll see you (I presume?) on the flight' – it all went quiet again.

I reckoned there was at best a 50 per cent chance this was all real, but there were worse things than finding myself in Sardinia for ten days in September with nothing to do. I got up early one morning, left my girlfriend a note – 'Out of cash – borrowed your credit card – back in ten days. Sorry!' – and went.

It worked. Gordon, middle-aged, a little greying, and surprisingly softly spoken for a skipper, picked me out of a crowded departure lounge at Gatwick. I don't know how he identified me. He gave me his bag to carry.

Porto Cervo is a synthetic, pseudo-classical Mediterranean fishing village. The 'Old Port' dates back to the 1960s, but most of it isn't nearly as ancient. It was built round a marina and the Yacht Club Costa Smerelda, probably the poshest yacht club in the world. Now, let's be clear, given the continued existence of the Royal Yacht Squadron and the New York Yacht Club, that's saying something. It's a resort for the very, very rich. The only people who even know it's there are very, very rich. Or carrying the bag of just such a person.

Gordon had rented a quite exceptionally small car, which the five of us who had been on the flight shared on the drive from the airport. As we neared Porto Cervo, a mis-diagnosis of deep-vein thrombosis from the back seat persuaded Gordon to stop and let us out for a moment, pulling onto the shoulder of a road along the cliff-tops overlooking the resort. The hot sun reflected off the sand-coloured rocks, but it was tempered by a breeze off the sea.

Down in the bay, a dozen yachts were racing in towards a buoy. They were all the enormous variety of racer known as a 'maxi-yacht', around the 100-foot mark.[28] These are the glamorous play-things of the extremely rich, invariably packed with an all-star crew, and about as far removed from the kind of sailing I'd been doing all year as the America's Cup was from Carrickfergus Sailing School.

[28] Bear in mind that a 100-foot boat is not merely twice the size of a 50-foot boat. The extra 50 feet of length isn't at the ends, it's in the middle, where it increases the volume and weight of the boat by much more than 100 per cent. A boat that's twice as long is probably effectively eight times the size. And cost.

These were the sailing equivalent of Hollywood A-listers who normally only exist on screens or in magazines. But here they were, involved in the mundane act of rounding a leeward mark. The vast spinnakers came down – on each boat squads of crew could be seen struggling to gather up thousands of square feet of sail and stuff it down a hatch so big that it could have had the tip of a ballistic missile poking through it. Left to my own devices, I would have sat in the baking sun and watched them all day.

Gordon's boat was of a slightly more modest scale, but no less lovely. *White Osprey* was built in 1981, but to a design from the mid 1970s. It was very different from the kind of boats I'd been racing so far that year – it would have been a bit dated even in my Belfast Lough days. Swans are never cutting-edge; that's not what they're for. *White Osprey* weighed over 19 tons, which meant she had been a big, heavy boat even when she was built. And of course the heavier a boat is the more slowly it goes, and the harder it is to deal with the pressure in the sails and on the sheets and halyards that drag it about the ocean.

You could see how much grunt was going to be involved from the boat's layout. There seemed to be winches everywhere – fourteen compared to the six that a contemporary boat would have. The deck fittings were substantial bits of engineering. This was going to be old-fashioned yachting. And it was going to be heavy work.

Worrying about all that would have to wait for a day or two, until I'd got over the culture shock that had started with my first glimpse of the maxi-yachts in the bay. I spent most of the first few days staring open mouthed around me.[29] If you took all the swishest, most expensive yachts from the London Boat Show, polished them up and decorated them with beautiful women sipping champagne, then anchored them off Porto Cervo, you'd have been asked to move them because they were making the place look cheap.

It wasn't just the maxis (which were actually there for the previous week's regatta) and it wasn't just the Swans – there was everything from the ultra-modern cruiser-racers made by Wally, which looked like floating stealth fighters, all the way back to beautiful old classics, like the 130-foot J-class yacht *Velsheda*, from the 1930s, whose varnish and brass-work shone with a rare lustre. It was hard to believe that something that looked so wonderful had been designed and built for something as brutal as racing. One of *Velsheda*'s crew told me that if they had a beer on board after racing, they weren't allowed to set it down anywhere in case it left a mark. Similarly, sails were not permitted below to avoid any salt-water marking of the interior. It would be, in so many respects, like sailing my parents' sideboard, except that my parents' sideboard would probably not have been fast enough to come second in class.

Finally, inevitably, there were the huge motor yachts, the kind of thing you see lined up in Monaco. One modestly understated number, like an iceberg with windows and a helipad, had both an armed guard and a

[29] That is presumably what I was doing on day two when I wheeled a trolley from the supermarket into Paul Cayard, the America's Cup skipper, causing him to drop his coffee. After he'd glared at me and walked off, I retrieved the paper cup complete with its half-inch of coffee, and took it triumphantly back to *White Osprey*, where no one else was even remotely interested.

staff entrance. In line with recent fashion, most of the motor yachts had had underwater LEDs fitted round the hull, so that at night they seemed to float on a pool of rippling blue light.

The ostentation didn't really spoil the attractiveness of the effect. In Porto Cervo, you had to ignore the issue of ostentation; it was a redundant concept. The whole place was devoted to conspicuous consumption – you had to get used to it or you wouldn't have been able to function at all. It was like being trapped in the pages of *Harper's Bazaar*.

Gordon and I assessed all this on the first afternoon from the rubber dinghy, when we took a circuitous route to the world's most expensive chandlery to buy a few bits of rope and a couple of shackles. Gordon blanched at being asked for a month's rent for a Central London flat in exchange for the contents of one plastic bag. But it was only eight times the normal price, and we got to go shopping in a chandlery that had been carved out of a single block of marble, and it seemed to me that was worth something.

We cruised back in the dinghy, and looked around the millions and millions of pounds' worth of boats, identifying famous sailors. This was a place where *White Osprey*, the same size as the biggest of the Belfast Lough boats in the 1980s, was a small boat. It was going to be an interesting week.

The last time I took a significant step up in my sailing career, it had been a disaster. When I outgrew my Mirror, aged about fifteen, I had a difficult decision about what to do next. I got it wrong.

If I wanted to stay at Carrickfergus the only option was to move to a Flying Fifteen, a 20-foot keelboat.[30] But Flying Fifteens were expensive, and keelboat sailing is usually a slightly more mature occupation. Buying one at the age of fifteen seemed a bit young-fogeyish. I'd only have been able to afford a distinctly second-hand one, and there was a clear performance difference between the good boats and the bad.

The other issue was crew – a Flying Fifteen was still a two-man boat, and I couldn't think of anyone I wanted to sail with. A cynical view might be that I couldn't think of anyone who would be grown-up enough and hence heavy enough to do the job, but who would be prepared to take orders from someone as mediocre as me. The cynical view would probably be right.

Whatever the reasoning, instead of a Flying Fifteen, I bought a single-handed Laser dinghy, number 132056, and moved my sailing to the other side of Belfast Lough at Ballyholme Yacht Club in Bangor.

Lasers are a strict one-design class; even the spars and sails are identical. It's racing boiled down to its most basic – it's not about the boat, it's about the sailor. The Laser fleet at Ballyholme was one of the most competitive in

[30] Designed by Uffa Fox, a most interesting man who is now largely forgotten outside sailing circles. He was a brilliant designer and builder of small boats, but was famous enough to appear on *This is Your Life*, mainly because of his associations with the royal family. (He sailed with Prince Philip and gave lessons to the children – no doubt he felt a small swell of pride when Prince Charles was given command of the rattiest minesweeper the Royal Navy could find, and dispatched to Scotland to look for mines.) He was also notable for minor eccentricities like destroying with a shotgun blast the front wheel of a cyclist who annoyed him, and re-enacting the Battle of Trafalgar with Prince Philip in the bar of a yacht club using small brass starting-canons.

Ireland — there were national champions, Olympic sailors, and quite a few good juniors. For a young, talented dinghy sailor on the up and up, it was a great idea. The perfect next step.

You'll have spotted the flaw, I'm sure. I didn't have the talent. I floundered. On my first race I floundered literally — unused to the rather smaller margin for error in a Laser, I spent most of my time with the boat upside down. Eventually the crew of the rescue boat just followed me (slowly) around the course, stopping every so often to help me turn the thing back over. They were very polite and patient, but I could see the laughter in their eyes turning to irritation. I was in tears by the time I finished, but at least the amount of time I was spending underwater meant that no one noticed.

I just couldn't sail the Laser. Ordinary everyday things, like bringing the boat ashore, were difficult. In a single-hander you have to leave the boat floating on its own for a moment while you get the little launching trolley from the shore. Whenever everyone else did this, the boat waited obediently. Whenever I did it the damn thing turned and bolted for the open sea and freedom, and the rescue boat had to go and fetch it for me. Since I was usually among the last finishers, there was normally a substantial audience available to view this. Sailing the Mirror had been a battle against the sarcastic wilfulness of Stephen Dobbs. In the Laser there was no crew to keep me humble, so *132056* stepped into the breach itself.

The first racing I did in the Laser was the winter series — cold, grey Sunday mornings, with the temperature dropping each weekend until we had to break the ice on the slipway to launch the boats. I learned to sail with the mainsheet between my teeth so I could sit on a hand to try to keep it warm. The hell with windshifts – by December I was deciding whether to tack by which hand was closer to going grey and snapping off. I began to miss the Mirror fleet at Carrickfergus. I almost began to miss Stephen Dobbs. Almost.

'Well, hello!' said a familiar voice as I arrived on the first Sunday morning in January. Dobbs was sitting cross-legged on a kit bag in the dinghy park, in the same revolting wetsuit bottoms that he'd been wearing since I'd first met him. 'And what's this?' he continued, turning to make a gosh-what's-that gesture at the shiny new Laser behind him. 'It's Stephen's new boat! God, I'm looking forward to this. This is going to be mega.'

It was a breezy day, and the water was cold. And, well, what can I say? Dobbs capsized within seconds of getting into his boat. In fact, it was kind of a smooth fluid motion – in one side, out the other. He turned it over another three times before the race started, and when it did start, who was that, upside down in the middle of the starting-line?

Dobbs had been right. It was mega. By the time I found him ashore after the race, he'd been backed into a corner by a slightly batty woman who was giving him a sermon on 'The first shall be last and the last shall be first'. Dobbs subjected to humiliation *and* religious hectoring. I made an obscene gesture at him behind the woman's back. It was one of my better days.

I did improve – by the following spring I'd become one of the better juniors, and could hold my own in the middle of the fleet. This meant I finally vanquished Dobbs on a regular basis. I should probably give myself some credit – I worked hard, I analysed races afterwards, and worked out what I'd done wrong. For me, it was quite mature.

Looking back, I reckon I was doing all right, but I was far too impatient to realise that at the time. All I could see then were boats in front of me, and I ended up in the same fury at my own mediocrity as I had in Carrickfergus. Scornfully, I sized up most of the people in front of me as mere hobby sailors, albeit it with some talent and, sometimes, years of experience. I was somehow entitled to be better than them, because, well, I wanted to be. The old gap between what I expected and what I was getting was still there. It meant that every day felt like an off day. I felt as if I sailed races composed entirely of mistakes. I'd have enjoyed my sailing a lot more if I'd looked at the boats behind, of which there were more than I imagined, but I never did.

In the end, though, what wrecked it, what made the whole Laser thing a mistake was that I was fifteen. My mobility was limited to how far I could ride a bike carrying a rudder, a centreboard, a tiller and a sail. And wearing a wetsuit, which was the real killer.[31] I couldn't actually get to Ballyholme unless someone gave me a lift, and unlike Carrickfergus, Dad wasn't going there anyway. In summer, when the club racing more or less stopped to make way for the various clubs' regattas, I had no easy means of transporting the boat to get to them. Laser sailing might have been the smart step up on my proposed trajectory, but the boat was sitting in a dinghy park 30 miles away.

[31] Especially with the famed sense of humour of the Northern Irish bystander to deal with – 'I hope we don't get the weather you're expecting!'

So I got the boat home to Lough Neagh, to practise my boat handling. To the inexperienced eye this looked a lot like going for laid-back sails on sunny summer afternoons. Sometimes I took my girlfriend, who was hardly relevant to boat-handling skills in a single-handed dinghy, but it was nice to have company.

Occasionally we took a picnic, and went to some distant, inaccessible shore. We would sit together on the little strip of sand and driftwood that separated the water from the forest, and talk about the future. It was all very pleasant, frankly a lot more pleasant than slogging through a winter series on Ballyholme Bay, but the sandwiches tasted of failure.

Most of my sailing from then on was back on the bigger boats at Carrickfergus, for no better reason than it was easy to get a lift there. I used to walk past the Flying Fifteens by the dock, and usually stopped there to say hello to the guys I had sailed Mirrors with. I used to tell them how great the Laser sailing was over in Ballyholme. And all my dreams slipped a little further away.

In case I'd forgotten what the dreams that sustained me through winter sailing on Belfast Lough looked like, they looked exactly like the first race at Porto Cervo. It was all there. Blue sea – astonishingly so. Blue sky. Perfect 12-knot breeze. Matching T-shirts. Shorts. Sunglasses. Photographers' helicopters, which I must admit I'd entirely omitted from the original fantasy, but which when you think about it are really a very necessary part of the tableau. Nothing says you've arrived like being followed by a helicopter, unless you're driving a stolen car.

I don't think we had any car thieves on *White Osprey*, but we had everything else. The crew had been cobbled together from two different boats, plus a few internet brides like me. This produced an outfit that was so mismatched in age, talent and attitude that when one morning one of the team stepped on board and announced in a Geordie accent, 'Day five on the Big Brother boat . . .' it seemed to sum it up perfectly.

For instance, the dream scenario didn't include a sixteen-year-old bowman whose determination to sail barefoot meant that when the going got tough, he could be relied upon to either fall over or stub his toe. All our manoeuvres were punctuated with thumps and bangs and swearing from the front of the boat.

On the other hand, we had Sir John, and I wouldn't have quite expected him either. He looked like a bricklayer, but was a former professional sailor, and could do almost everything better than any of the rest of us, from re-wiring the electrics to trimming the sails. He knew where the line was, what time it was, and he didn't fall over. (There was informed speculation that his knighthood may have stemmed from an evening drinking with the governor of a Caribbean island, and thus might not be completely watertight from a legal point of view. But it was a godsend for getting restaurant reservations in Porto Cervo.)

And so it went on – from a rock-hard bruiser called Oz to a grinder who started the week looking like an especially well-groomed banker and finished it wearing a bloodstained T-shirt and a bandana, looking like he ought to have been emerging from the jungle with a machine gun.

We were eighth in the first race, out of a class of more than forty. We were pleased with that, and a little surprised, but we reckoned we could do better. Ironically, I was too busy gazing around me to really care. The course took us up round the north of Sardinia, in and out of the rocks and islets and over towards Corsica. I'd seen this backdrop so many times – pictures of big boats racing here had been a staple of magazine photo spreads for thirty years. It had always seemed just too stereo-typical – a group of rocky islands drawn by a five-year-old, surrounded by blue, blue water. But here it all was, like running onto the pitch at Wembley. I couldn't believe how like the rocks of northern Sardinia the rocks of northern Sardinia looked. It was just bloody fantastic.

The second race had incidents. We got a good start, but in a gybe shortly afterwards we had a foul-up that took some minutes to clear. Afterwards, I suggested to Owen – like me, part of the mast/bow team – that we ought to set the spinnaker pole up differently. I'll be honest, Owen annoyed the hell out of all of us. He was a twenty-year-old know-all who wanted to be a pro. He was a very good sailor, but without wishing to be uncharitable, he had the personality of something you'd scrape off your shoe. He came over as arrogant and rude, and seemed to be absolutely convinced of his own brilliance.[32]

'That's the way I always do it,' said Owen.

'Well, since it didn't work, maybe we should try it a different way. It's an old boat, so why don't we give the old-style set-up a shot,' I said.

'Listen, I was told to do it that way by the best bowman

---

[32] You should hear me when I'm being uncharitable.

in England. Are you the best bowman in England? I don't fucking think so. I'm going to do it that way. That's the best way.'

'Except it doesn't work. The end of the pole is the wrong shape.'

'Fuck off, just fuck off.'

When the next gybe went the same way, John told me to change the set-up. I asked Owen if he had a roll of PVC tape I could use. He took it out of a pocket, contemplated it for a moment, looked up, then hurled it at my face as hard as he could. I dodged, and the tape landed in the sea.

'Hey, Michael!' Oz tossed me a roll of tape, and scowled at Owen. Owen was even more upset when the old way worked better than his.

The wind built in strength through the morning. Eventually, as the wind funnelled down an island sound, Gordon called for a spinnaker change. This went perfectly smoothly, right up to the point where we hoisted the new sail.

At this point I need to introduce Katie. Her contribution to the sailing was not extensive, but all the available evidence suggested there was a rule in Sardinia requiring an attractive girl in a bikini to be on board at all times, and Katie was ours. She was fortunate enough to have a rich father, and at the point where she enters our story she had just graduated with a 2.1 degree. With no apparent need to look for a career, she was trying to decide whether to become a hostess on a super-yacht or devote a few years to her three-day eventing.

Fans of karma may guess what's coming next. Katie was sitting on the side-deck during the hoist, applying suntan lotion. Specifically, she was inadvertently sitting on the new spinnaker sheet, which as the sail filled with wind twanged taut, like a bow-string.

In the process it launched Katie.

Upwards and outwards she flew, with an expression on her face that was probably entirely representative of everyone who has ever suffered an unexpected conversion from sunbather to projectile. She was still holding the suntan lotion bottle.

I had an excellent view of the whole thing. As Katie described a flailing parabola high into the air, I thought, 'Well, at least the water's warm.' Not totally facetious; at least she wouldn't die of hypothermia while we, or more likely someone behind us, picked her up.

The next thing I thought (she was up there for quite a while) was, 'Damn, if we don't get her back, we'll be disqualified.' The rules, not unreasonably, are pretty clear that you have to finish the race with the same number of crew you started with. You can't throw away the ones you don't like.[33]

The third thing I thought was, 'Maybe I should nip over and try to catch her.'

The fourth was, 'Isn't it quiet without her?'

Katie, to her considerable credit, did what I certainly wouldn't have had the reflexes to do, which was to catch

---

[33] The exception to this is Bermuda fitted-dinghy racing, where there is no such rule. In lightening winds it's common for surplus crew to jump off. Bermuda fitted-dinghy racing is a fairly gonzo activity – the boats are wildly unstable and prone to capsize, and have very low freeboards, so they have a distinct tendency towards filling with water. They only stay afloat because crew members bail them out continuously, which means you have to be careful not to discard too many of them.

the sheet on her way back down. In spite of dislocating her shoulder, she hung on, dangling several feet out over the water. I was closest to her, but I was still making fast the halyard from the hoist. Letting go to grab Katie would have resulted in the spinnaker coming down, with it the sheet Katie was hanging on to, and on top of her, the sail itself. In the end it was Oz who hauled her back on board, and Katie herself who popped her shoulder back into its socket (eurgh!).

Katie was lucky – not that she caught the sheet, again, that was down to her – but that the sheet ejected her from the boat cleanly. If it had looped round an ankle or a wrist, it could have been nasty. Even if we exclude drowning (which, technically, is usually the result of bad swimming, not bad sailing) you can kill yourself in a variety of ways, most of which I've pointed out in this book in an attempt to make the whole enterprise seem a little more macho.

Short of major disasters, even normal sailing can hurt. If you're working the bow or mast areas, you always hurt yourself a bit – bumps, bruises, pulled muscles. After a windy regatta as a bowman, you feel like you've been given a light beating. Some things hurt for quite a long time. I tore a tendon in my wrist in Tarbert that I can still feel twinging today. And I have a Z-shaped scar on my forehead (very fashionable) from getting hit in the face by *Blaze of Glory*'s spinnaker pole at the national championships. One of the crew on that occasion was an A & E doctor who yelped as blood flew everywhere, and as a prelude to anything more useful screamed, 'For fuck's sake, don't bleed on the sails; Mac will kill you.' I was stitched back together on the next upwind leg by Sarah, an ex-army nurse, who held me still by kneeling on my chest.

Katie's adventure may have looked spectacular, but it didn't slow us down. We were third in race two. That put us fourth overall. All things considered, we were doing rather well. Despite the random nature of the personnel, the crew work was astonishingly crisp – we did one spinnaker peel (a tricky manoeuvre involving two spin-nakers, most of the ropes on the boat, and an especially lavish number of ways to balls it all up) that was so sharp we got a round of applause from the nearby boats.

Given how prone to sulking I am, I was pretty proud of how well Owen and I worked together, despite not being able to stand the sight of each other – since we were the two most experienced members of the team at the front of the boat, we had to at least avoid the easy temptation of making life hard for each other. It was probably the closest approach I made to real personal growth all year.

The same couldn't necessarily be said for Oz, who entertained the same warm feelings for Owen that I did. In one manoeuvre, Owen got a crack on the head from the heavy shackle on the end of a swinging halyard. 'Shit!' said Oz. I was surprised he was so concerned. 'Nah, fuck him,' Oz went on. 'I'm just pissed off it took me three goes. Hitting a head that size should have been easy.'

If we worked as a team on the boat, it was different ashore. There were two camps – those who were sleeping in a nearby apartment complex, and those on the boat. I was on the boat, sleeping in only moderate discomfort, in a berth with a (unprecedented in my career) sprung mattress.

Sleeping on board meant I was close to the luxurious amenities of the Yacht Club Costa Smerelda – its cool marble atrium, its expensive art works, its classy, understated decoration and its azure-coloured swimming pool. I could admire it each morning as I shuffled past in the world's most uncomfortable flip-flops (purchased from the chandlery for only €40) on my way to the shit-hole (and I mean that in the most literal way) that was the shower and toilet block for people who were indigent enough to be sleeping on a boat in Porto Cervo.

I did, one morning, seeing the entrance unguarded, slip into the club, into its downstairs gents, and, like a nervous burglar, into a cubicle. I say cubicle from habit – it was about the size of my living room, in muted shades of brown and beige, with gentle lighting. There were polished fittings, fluffy towels, and a toilet bowl in the far corner. I got the feeling that after I left, the whole room would be snapped off the block like a square of chocolate, and replaced with a new one.

That was as far as any of us sleeping on board penetrated into the club. But Gordon, as skipper, attended numerous parties. We ran into him one night as we checked the result board in the piazza in front of the club – us in our T-shirts and grubby shorts, Gordon and his wife in evening wear. It was slightly uncomfortable. The whole organisation of the event had a hint of 'the owners' and 'the crew'.

On *White Osprey* the class distinctions extended to the internal arrangements, at least when the boat was on the dock. The four of us sleeping on board ended up charged with the cleaning and upkeep of the boat – everyone else seemed to wander off to the apartment for a shower and didn't come back. We also took responsibility for provisioning, wheeling a supermarket trolley a quarter of a mile back to the boat, being honked at by a stream of passing Ferraris and Maseratis as we went, then taking the trolley back to get the one-euro deposit. At least, in the warm morning sun, it wasn't the hardship it would have been in, say, Carrickfergus.

Gordon was always a little miffed if he arrived in the morning and found that we were still eating breakfast on deck. He was justly proud of his boat, and I fear he thought we were making it look untidy. It wasn't exactly fair, but on the other hand it didn't really seem worth arguing about. You could tell that he didn't relish the contrast we presented with the boat next door, a swishy, well-funded and probably substantially professional outfit. I imagine he was a little pained one morning when that crew arrived in smart matching kit, in a gleaming crew mini-bus, just as I was gathering in the underpants I'd put in the rigging overnight to dry.

The demand that we fix the heads, left blocked by one of the apartment sleepers, was a bit much. We didn't actually refuse to do it; we just found lots of other things to do first. Eventually Gordon got exasperated, and did the job himself. It was a small victory, but one that we shouldn't have celebrated by telling an official who arrived on the dock that the skipper was down below, 'going through the motions'. When Gordon subsequently came on deck in a pair of pink rubber gloves, keeping a straight face was, sadly, impossible.

We had a gas leak one night too. Or at least, the gas alarm went off at 4 a.m. It was very loud, very piercing, and it wouldn't stop. After careful consideration and

217

some anxious sniffing, we voted by a 3–1 majority to smash it to bits with a winch-handle and go back to bed. This didn't impress Gordon either. When he arrived in the morning, he instructed us to ensure there were, in fact, no leaks. It was also his opinion that gas, being heavier than air, might have accumulated invisibly in the bilges, awaiting its chance to blow *White Osprey* to bits. We were told to make sure that any such gas was removed, while Gordon attended to some urgent business a long, long way from the boat.

There is a pleasingly absurd standard procedure for this. We took turns to scoop the purported gas out of the bilges with a bucket, pass it carefully through the companionway hatch, pour the resulting bucketful of nothing at all over the side of the boat, and pass the bucket back. It was surprisingly relaxing, even if it was hard to know when we'd finished.

There were compensations to sleeping on the boat. For a start, we were at all times near the bar of the co-sponsors, Peroni. This served free beer. All day, every day, as much as you wanted, to anyone who chanced by. A considerable perk – though the take-up was modest among most of the crews. Despite the hundreds of sailors hanging about, you rarely saw much of a queue. I wouldn't want to trade in national stereotypes, but I'm well aware that if you gave away free beer in Cowes, half of Southampton would swim the Solent to get to it.

The best thing of all for someone like me was that there were lots of professional yachties about. Men who lived out the old moth-eaten dreams I kept for years in my parents' loft. We shared the shit-hole showers; we drank beer at the Peroni bar. ('It's OK, lads, I'll get this round.')

I kept hoping I'd find my mirror image – the sailor who had wanted to be a cyclist.

After a few days, I could kind of kid myself that I was one of them. I'd done enough sailing to have stories to swap, but more importantly I didn't pretend to be something I wasn't, and I was smart enough to listen more than I talked.

Unlike the amateurs, most of the pros' conversation wasn't about manoeuvres that had gone wrong, or expensive bits of gear that exploded in a shower of carbon-fibre. For them, fuck-ups weren't funny; fuck-ups cost money. They talked business; where were they going next? Did they have a boat for the southern hemisphere regattas over the European winter, or were they going to the US? Who had a project that needed personnel? It was exactly the conversation I'd had every year as a full-time cyclist. Who had a team needing riders? What events were they going to do? You had to pick right – get it wrong, and you'd end up not getting paid, or committed to attempting things you couldn't do, and then have a hell of a job getting back into an outfit that wasn't just going to stiff you.

I was flattered when one of them asked me if I was planning to go to the Voiles de St Tropez, an invitation-only event in early October, packed out with the smartest and most expensive boats afloat. It was where quite a few of the boats were heading after the Swan Cup was over. I said no, no chance. People like me didn't go to the Voiles. 'You should; you'd like it,' he said. 'It's even more up its own arse than this place.' He laughed and wrote a name and a phone number on a bit of paper, saying, 'Here, give Steve a call. He'll get you set up.'

And, just like that, a different world beckoned. I folded the bit of paper and put it in a pocket, just like the scribbled phone number I'd been given fourteen years earlier that had unexpectedly marked my abandonment of sailing. Now, as then, I thought no more about it. Well, not much anyway. I was careful to remember which pocket I'd stuffed it into though.

The results kept coming – we scored a fourth, and in the final race, a fifth. We had one frustration in the penultimate race when we were over the line at the start – something that was obvious to half the boat, but not, sadly, visible to the helmsman, nor apparent to the bowman. I don't know how he missed it. I called us over the line from the mast, but Owen agreed with the bowman, I think to piss me off as much as anything else, and shouted loudly enough that the guys at the back believed him. It was lucky for us that the series rules discarded your worst result when the scores were totalled.

We ended up fifth over all. For a loosely scrabbled-together crew like ours, on a boat that rarely raced, it was a good result. Considering that ten days earlier when I left home I'd worried about whether the whole enterprise was the figment of someone else's imagination it was a triumph.

I'd been right all those years ago as well. The sunglasses, the T-shirts and shorts, the sun beating down – it had felt good. Very good. Transplanted to the warm breezes of the Mediterranean, sailing as pleasure suddenly made a lot more sense than it ever had on a January morning on Belfast Lough. When I looked back at those days from Porto Cervo, I found I couldn't really remember them very clearly.

I did know that the last ten days had been the best sailing I'd ever done. All right, so I hadn't been behind the wheel, the way the fantasies that played in my head during double chemistry required, but stuff it. I'd gone pretty close, and I didn't feel inclined to be picky. I was sorry it was over.

If I'd felt that I was sailing in the pages of one of my old magazines, a few weeks later I got the proof. One of them published a picture of *White Osprey* among the rocky islets, on one of the windier races, with the blue sea and sky, and the rugged backdrop. It looked fantastic.

Chapter Eleven

Helisara

THE FIRST NATIONAL TITLE I EVER WON MAY COME AS a surprise to you. It was at the Scottish All-Comers' Downstairs Diving Championships, held on the staircase of a hotel in Oban on the west coast of Scotland. I admit that it is possible that this event was not actually sanctioned by the world governing body of downstairs diving. But I don't care. I was the best on the day, and somewhere I still have the pint tankard nicked from the hotel bar that constituted the trophy. I remember that when presented it was filled with a strange, sweet-smelling green liquid that I was required to drink in one. After that, it all gets a bit hazy.

Downstairs diving is a simple sport. You stand at the top of a long flight of stairs, and dive off. If you do it with enough commitment, your angle of descent coincides with the angle of the staircase, so you land smoothly, sustaining only a couple of broken ribs and carpet-burned nipples. It's critical to remain relaxed, which is just one of the reasons it's best done drunk. Like ski jumping, it's scored for distance and style. My style was poor, but as I face-planted directly in the lobby without once touching the stairs, my distance was untouchable. My effort got a drunken roar of approval, and the longest round of applause I've ever received. It was, quite genuinely, a proud moment. Certainly it was a greater success than any I've enjoyed sailing.

I was unable to defend my title the following year, since I was subsequently chased from the hotel for taking an illicit shower – the old yachtie's trick of sauntering into a hotel, trying bedroom doors until you find one unlocked, and popping in for a quick spruce-up. Normally it works fine. On this occasion, however, I was rumbled, and pursued down the gridded steps of a metal fire escape, wearing only my underpants, by a distinctly irritated hotel manager. He didn't catch me, no mean achievement by me, considering I was barefoot. He didn't formally tell me I was banned either, but it seemed implicit in his final shouted words, 'If I ever see you in my hotel again I'll rip your head off.'

I hadn't gone to Oban specifically for the Championships. Like the kind of chap in the early years of the modern Olympics who almost inadvertently ended up winning a medal while they were on their holidays, I had really gone for West Highland Week. It wasn't a very prestigious event, but it was one of the few that took place in the school holidays. By that late in the season quite a few boats had trouble with their regular crew, who'd used up their holiday entitlement or were on a beach somewhere with their families. There was always space for a teenager with time on his hands.

Each year, after a day or two based in Oban, the Week

moved on to Tobermory, on the island of Mull. Tobermory has recently been best known as the dolly-mixture coloured location for the TV show *Balamory*, and hence is the toddler tourist hotspot *de nos jours*. Then it was notorious for pissed yachties, a heaving pub by the harbour called the Mishnish, casual sex, and the Fat Pat, a cocktail of equal measures Baileys liqueur and Irish whiskey.[34] (Since the event still happens, I assume these worlds collide each year, which sounds like fun. I would have gone again to see, but it clashed with Cowes Week.)

My life's one and only threesome happened in Tobermory. I was sleeping one night when I was woken by the mainsail trimmer and his girlfriend fumbling with each other and making drunken expressions of undying horniness in the bunk that was above and to one side of mine. They must have climbed over me to get to it.

Since I was only about fifteen, I was, I'll admit, mildly interested. I grew less enthusiastic when they fell out of their bunk and onto me. They didn't notice. I was unsure quite how to draw their attention to this – it was a tricky point of etiquette for which life had left me unprepared. So I lay there, pinned to the bunk, trying to work out if I was losing my virginity, or just getting stains on my sleeping bag.

By far the most memorable thing that happened to me

---

[34] The Mishnish was of such note that I once found myself in Glasgow Queen's Street station in a ticket queue behind a man looking for a ticket 'to Mishnish'. The ticket clerk sold him a ticket to Oban and told him to catch the ferry to Mull without missing a beat. The Fat Pat is highly recommended too. And my compliments to the local man who, asked by a pre-school *Balamory* fan if his was the house where Josie Jump lived, said it had been, but he'd killed her and buried her in the garden.

during West Highland Week was the unexpected result of the boat I was on breaking its mast. For most of the crew, that meant a disappointing early end to the week, and a long dreary trip home under engine. I decided I'd stay in Tobermory and take my chances. I had no boat, no crew, and not even anywhere to sleep. I was young enough to find this very, very exciting. As the rest of the crew motored off I waved an enthusiastic goodbye. I wasn't even too worried when I realised I'd left my wallet on board. That only made my situation more pleasingly dramatic. Down and out in *Balamory*; a middle-class parable of landing on your feet.

Within a few hours I'd borrowed some cash off a mate of my father's, taken it to the Mishnish, and invested the lot in buying drink for a gang of strangers from a boat called *Helisara*. They said I could come sailing with them for the rest of the week. 'Yeah, why not, we always need mushrooms,' were the exact words of the crew boss. I wasn't sure what this meant, but I didn't care. The plan had worked. A dream was about to come to life.

Helisara, you see, was a maxi-yacht. Eighty feet long, which in those days was as big as the rules allowed a racing-yacht to be, she was the kind of boat that until that moment had only existed in my magazines and fantasies. I don't know how she ended up racing a mediocre series in Tobermory. She was ten years old, and a bit tired-looking, but she was still a star, and should have been in the Mediterranean. It was like finding an ageing Hollywood sex-symbol in the local amateur dramatic club.[35]

---

[35] This impression was not in any way undermined by her previous owner having been Herbert von Karajan.

You can guess how much this bothered me. The boat was in Scotland, and I was in the boat. I'd been issued with my T-shirt (well, I nicked one that was drying on a life-line), and I was one of sailing's most envied men, a maxi-sailor. It was an ironic counterpoint to my manifest lack of success in proper sailing – dinghies – that here I was on one of the most prestigious yachts in Britain, part of a vast twenty-man crew.

I was not doing one of the more glamorous jobs. A mushroom, it turned out, was the name for the guys who worked below decks, packing sails, living in perpetual twilight, and having crap thrown at them.

There were three of us: me, a girl called Mary, and our leader, Stu. Stu was only a little older than me, and had originally planned to spend his summer on a sail-training vessel run by a charity. But he'd met the *Helisara* guys in Plymouth while he was, literally, waiting for his ship to come in. They'd been short of crew. When Stu said no, they spiked his drink and kidnapped him. He woke up, feeling like death, in the bowels of the maxi and heading for Scotland.

The rest of the crew realised their mistake when he came to and started talking. His most favoured topic was his car, which he'd parked on a Plymouth back street and could not remember locking. His conversation was, as a result, repetitive: 'I remember locking it, but then I had to go back and get my bag from the boot, and I don't think I locked it again. I really don't. Oh Christ, it'll be nicked. It's only insured third party. Shit, shit, shit.'

So while on deck the rest of the crew trimmed sails, made tactical decisions, and worked on their suntans, beneath their feet, in a gloomy underworld of aluminium ring-frames and bracing, the three of us worked non-stop to haul used spinnakers and headsails in through the huge fore-hatch, fold them, bag them, put them away, and always be ready to provide whatever sail the guys upstairs demanded next.

It was hard, hard physical work. One of *Helisara*'s spinnakers was about 5,000 square feet, and it took the three of us about twenty minutes to pack. The spinnakers weren't just stuffed into bags, they were zipped into full-length nylon tubes designed to keep the sail under control until it was fully hoisted. Then the zip was broken, and the sail popped open. It made life easy on deck, and hell below.

To get the sails into the tube, we had to lay them out as straight as we could along the floor, through a series of bulkheads, slipping and sliding and falling on the fabric as the boat heeled one way and then the other. When we had everything straight, Stu pulled the zip-fastener along the 100-foot length of the tube while Mary and I tried to hold it closed ahead of him. It was always a tight fit, like zipping an anaconda into a too-small evening dress.

Both headsails and spinnakers usually came down the hatch accompanied by a waterfall. There were days when the only people on board wearing oilskins were the mushrooms, losing half their body-weight in sweat, almost forgotten in the sewer. We were disconnected from the actual sailing – one race saw a major panic on deck as a headsail sheet jammed on the winch, leaving the boat thundering towards the rocks with no safe means of stopping her. Eventually the bravest man in the crew was dispatched to cut the wire-rope sheet, under tons of load, with bolt croppers. On deck there were white faces and shaky knees. In the sewer below, the three of us worked away, because down there everything was quite normal.

It was hard to kid myself that this was, taken on its own terms, actually fun. But it was worth it for the moments of peace, and for the sheer glamour. On one long passage race back to Oban we finally got to go on deck, and sit on the rail with the rest of the crew. The biggest boats had started last (the second biggest was a mere 50 feet) and we just roared past the smaller boats. On every single one of them someone produced a camera. Most of us spent the race smiling and waving for pictures, as if on a red carpet laid down the Sound of Mull. I smiled so hard my face hurt. Stu, his heart still miles away with his ancient Mini, dolefully told me this condition was called the 'maxi-grin'.

I have a wonderful haze of memories from that week. Sailing back to harbour after a race in the evening sun, standing with Stu and Mary in the open fore-hatch, drinking a lager and looking at the colourful houses behind Tobermory quay. Or the prank we played one drunken night in Oban, where we sent one of the crew into a pub walking on his knees. He ordered twenty pints. When they were lined up, he turned to the door and sang, 'Hi-ho!' Then the rest of us marched in on our knees, singing, 'It's off to work we go.' We did this in two pubs, but that wasn't the joke. The joke was when we sent Stu into a rough-looking fishermen's bar on his knees, and everyone else went to the pub across the road and left him in an unamused silence, with twenty beers he couldn't pay for, shouting 'Hi-ho' at the door.

Most of all I remember what it was like to race such a big, demanding boat, to be part of such a big team. I was keen enough to make a good impression that I worked hard. I helped with the dull jobs as well as the racing – deck scrubbing, making twenty packed-lunches, helping to fix the numerous broken bits of maxi. I fitted in well enough that the skipper took my details to add me to the list of regulars – since Stu wasn't willing to come back it was even implied that next time I would be King of the Mushrooms, and wear the zip-fastener of office on a string round my neck.

The irony was that the whole experience just underlined how badly my sailing career was going. I have already pointed out the distinction on bigger boats between the brains and the humble mechanicals. On *Helisara* that distinction was more hard-edged than ever. The analogy that seemed most appropriate was Formula 1 – we start with the skipper who, like the driver, gets his name on the trophy. Then there are several other members of the afterguard, who are like the blokes who sit in the pits making important decisions about when to fill the car with petrol. We have sail trimmers, who tune the engine. And we have blokes who hold the wheel-nuts during the pit stop. I was a dab hand with the wheel-nuts. But the painful truth is that the wheel-nut-bloke is less important than the actual wheel-nut.

I was a good mushroom. It required only hard work, organisation and a certain physical fitness. Talent wasn't on the spec-sheet. But being a mushroom had very little to do with sailing. Nothing in my dog-eared library of tactics books was relevant here. The hours I spent with Stephen Dobbs could have been a different sport entirely.

Helisara might have been a foot in the door of the pro scene. But it wasn't really the way I wanted it. I'd slid into more and more big-boat sailing as my dinghying career stalled, because just being on board and part of the team seemed like the next best thing. But it wasn't. When you're a mushroom, the stars are so far above you that they may as well not exist at all.

At the time, I thought that maybe I could have been a pro, or something that looked very like it. But only the kind of jobbing pro who trekked around Europe with his life in a kit bag, sleeping in foul-smelling boats and surviving on the charity of rich boat owners, while the bastards with the actual talent got the money and the glory. I would spend more time sanding down the bottoms of boats and scrubbing decks than I ever would sailing. The only thing separating such a life from unemployed homelessness would have been the free T-shirts. And if the thinness of the shirts on *Helisara* was anything to go by, they wouldn't keep you warm for long.

Without any chance of personal glory, was it something I'd do anyway? Well, perhaps. But suddenly I wasn't sure that I loved sailing enough. It was the first doubt of that kind I'd ever had. What with the towering evidence of my continuing mediocrity, I was no longer convinced that I was good enough to be a star. It was a triumph for blind optimism that I had ever been convinced of it at all. But at least I had always known that sailing was the best thing in the world, and worth giving a lot for. Just, it now turned out, not everything.

As it was, I was spared the decision. *Helisara* disappeared from the Scottish scene not long afterwards, presumably because whoever bought her couldn't afford to run her. I don't know where she went. The chance slipped away before it had really solidified. And that was the end of that.

*

Nice airport was almost deserted. The woman behind the Tourist Information desk peered at me over the top of a pair of wire-rimmed glasses that had clearly been carefully selected to give her a frosty appearance, and hopefully put tourists off asking for information. 'Monsieur?' she said. I repeated my question.

'Monsieur,' she said, 'no one arrives in St Tropez by bus. You can go by helicopter . . .' She took a leaflet out of a holder, looked at my horrified expression, and put it back again. 'Or you can rent a car. Or you can catch a bus to somewhere else.'

I rented a car, and drove it down the Cote d'Azure with all the windows open, and warm autumn air blowing round me. I'd left a rainy October in London behind me, and I was on my way to the Voiles de St Tropez. I was happy with the world.

St Tropez was a little odd. For a start, it was smaller than I had expected. There was clearly a lot of money about – flash cars, designer shops, things that felt exclusive – but also a lot of tourists and tourist tat.

The mix was most striking down at the old harbour. It was filled with the world's swishest yachts. Many of them had come straight from Porto Cervo. They were joined by half a dozen floating museums' worth of classic yachts, boats that demanded several full-time crew just to keep their woodwork varnished and the brass polished. But unlike Porto Cervo, St Tropez harbour wasn't a rich-man's hideaway. The quaysides were thronged several-deep with spectators, just gazing at the millionaires' toys and seeing money. Having a damned good look at how the other half live. I suppose the millionaires could have looked back and enjoyed the reverse experience. For the most part they didn't.

The antiques included, in a nice touch from my perspective, Herbert von Karajan's first *Helisara*. It was smaller but more elegant than the boat I'd sailed on, which had been von Karajan's sixth of the name. That had been a big metal beast of a boat. This was lovely, glowing varnish and deep lustrous paintwork. Since I was wearing my *Helisara* T-shirt – I thought it might make an interesting talking point at an event full of classic boats even if it was a bit scruffy – I went to introduce myself to the crew. But trying to explain why a man they'd never seen was wearing a shirt with the name of their boat on it was beyond my linguistic skills. They thought I was some kind of maritime stalker. Unfortunately, telling them I used to be '*un champignon*' when I was younger didn't make them think I was any less crazy.

In this idyllic setting, the life of the professional seemed not so bad. Which was good news, since that's what I'd come for. To finally catch up on the chance that had slipped past, and to see if I'd been right to let it go. In the same way that my teenage sailing had led to *Helisara*, my comeback year had led to this.

I'd spoken to Steve a couple of times the previous week, and he'd found me a place on one of the big, hi-tech Wally yachts, over 100 feet in length. Looking at the boat in question in the harbour, it seemed even bigger. The deck was like a teak football field, and like all big yachts, it sat rock-steady – when you move around on a smaller boat, tidying up like the crew on the Wally were doing, it moves from side to side a little. This thing behaved more like an island.

Steve was in his forties, a little greying, and altogether older than I'd expected. He was living with his girlfriend in St Tropez, for the moment at least. From the way he described it, I wasn't sure how permanent any of Steve's homes had been. He had the appealing air of a bohemian drifter. He took me up the passerelle of my ride for the week to introduce me to the skipper, Wayne.[36]

'What?' said Wayne.

Steve reminded him of a conversation they'd had the previous week, about my joining the crew.

'Don't think so, mate. Who is he anyway?'

I explained, mentioning my maxi experience, my dinghying background (which is always a plus, even if you weren't much good, because it at least proves you know how a sailing boat works), and the Swan Worlds. It felt like a pretty decent CV when I said it with conviction and avoided the word 'mushroom'. Wayne was unmoved.

'Nah, sorry, we're not really looking for anyone.'

'No worries,' said Steve, and took me to meet the skipper of another boat.

'No, got all we need.'

'Easy,' said Steve, and led me round to another boat. 'We'll ask Nigel.'

'Get off my boat,' said Nigel.

After half an hour of rejection, it became clear that Steve had asked everyone he knew.

'We'll go and have a few beers tonight – something will turn up,' he said.

---

[36] A passerelle is what you call a gang-plank if you don't want to sound like a tourist.

In the end, even Steve didn't turn up. I got a text saying he had to go to a crew party, where everyone was under orders to be happy and smiling for the owner. Instead, he suggested, I could have dinner with his girlfriend, which was a bit on the odd side, I suppose, but it beat going out on my own. Which is how I came to spend the evening in a Vietnamese restaurant with a German ex-model, the ex-wife of the town's ex-mayor. When we caught up with Steve in a bar later, he assured me that he'd got something sorted out for the following day.

Next morning, Steve's mobile was turned off. Eventually I gave up looking for him, and went on a tour of the harbour, asking if anyone wanted crew. I asked at *French Kiss*, the former America's Cup boat, and at *Challenge Twelve*, the boat that had been the training partner of *Australia 2*. I asked at *Velsheda*. I asked at *Cotton Blossom*, the classic owned by Dennis Conner, the skipper defeated in the '83 America's Cup, and the man who won it back in '87. So many childhood heroes. They all said no.

I asked at a couple of the Swans, hoping to meet someone from Porto Cervo. No. I asked at any other boat that had crew about. No, no. Sorry, but no. I tried the huge yacht owned by the CEO of L'Oréal, just so I could say, 'But I washed my hair specially!' when they said no. (In one of the great missed opportunities, the boat wasn't called *Because I'm Worth It*. It was called *Magic Carpet Squared*. I don't know what it means either.)

This was not going the way I'd planned it. I hadn't come all the way to St Tropez to stand on the harbour wall but that's what I seemed to be doing. It looked like a disappointing way for my last trip of the year to finish.

Eventually I asked at another of the Wallys. They said no, but that if I fancied it, I could help out on the tender: 'Frank could do with a bit of company.' It was the closest thing I'd seen to a chink of light, so I said yes.

The tender was a fast rigid-inflatable powerboat, in which Frank and I had the job of following the yacht out, and collecting the huge heavy mooring warps and fenders, and whatever sails the skipper decided he wouldn't need for the day, then bringing them ashore. Then we dashed out again after the boat to collect the owner's wife, and take her ashore. Then back out to the boat. I'd taken a step down from holding the wheel-nuts, a step that I didn't know existed. Now I was a van driver's mate, but at least I was a van driver's mate in the warm sun, with wind in my hair, and the world's most extravagant yachts to look at.

Frank and I chased the racing all day. Upwind, downwind, bouncing from wave to wave, dodging the boats as they tacked or gybed, and avoiding the other tenders doing the same thing. We had to shout to each other over the noise of the engine, and the clatter of helicopters overhead.

I was never quite sure what we were all there for, what use we actually served. Maybe it was just so that the big boats and their rich owners always had someone on hand to look at them admiringly.

Or perhaps it was just to be humbled. Steering the boat we were chasing was a man called Chris Law. He'd been a star since before I could remember – I was almost as disappointed when he finished outside the medals at the 1984 Olympics as he was. He'd been the helmsman of the British America's Cup boat in 1987, in which capacity he had actually been on a poster on my bedroom wall.

Now, he stood behind the wheel of the 100-foot Wally, steering with precise, definite movements. It was like watching a master craftsman. Elite performers in any sport have an air of confidence. It's almost a glow, like they're lit from within. Gery had steered *Moorish Idol* a lot like that, but Law was better. I could have watched him all day, not because I thought I'd learn anything, just to see it being done so close to perfectly.[37]

The rest of the crew was the same. Mistakes just didn't happen. Spinnakers went up, and came down with no fuss at all. Sail changes happened quickly and accurately. Sails were trimmed perfectly – the trimmers continually made small adjustments, maybe just an inch or two on a sail several thousand square feet in area. I knew that's how sails were supposed to look, but I could spend all day tweaking and never manage it. There is some sort of deep talent for it, some ability to feel what's right, what the wind wants, how the boat moves, and how to tweak two or three bits of rope to make it happen.

The night before, in the bar, Steve had told me about a friend of his who'd blagged his way onto a top boat a couple of years previously – a man who'd won national sailing titles, so a good sailor, probably better than anyone (apart from Gery) I'd ever crewed with. On one beat the headsail trimmer managed to injure himself, so Steve's mate took over for a few moments. He hadn't had the sheet in his hand for more than a couple of seconds, and had made exactly no adjustments to anything, before the

---

[37] Sadly, Law died in 2007.

skipper, without even looking over, barked, 'Would one of you get whatever prick is trimming the headsail off the winch and get someone who knows what they're doing?'

As Frank and I bounced along in the tender, I remembered sitting in the café at Porto Cervo, listening to the pro sailors talking the same language as pro cyclists. Watching Law and his crew, another similarity was uncomfortably apparent: most amateur cyclists and fans have no idea just how good the 'ordinary' pros are. They know the stars are good – but they assume that if the stars can hammer the journeyman pros, that the journeymen can't be that much better than the amateurs. They're wrong. The struggling pro that they make jokes about for being a bit of a donkey would hammer them in any kind of race they chose.

I'd fallen into the same trap. These guys were fantastic. I hadn't even realised it could be done this well. I'd always imagined that top-class sailing was like what I'd been doing for a large proportion of my life, just better. I'd even be prepared to stretch to a lot better. In sad reality it was a whole different thing.

So here's the irony. I'd spent the season discovering that I was a better racing sailor than I'd thought. I'd gone back to my childhood and teenage years, and revised everything upwards a little. After years of looking back and regretting all the things I didn't do because I was too busy bickering with Stephen Dobbs and bobbing about on a sea of sewage, it was nice to discover I'd gained something along the way other than a nice line in sarcasm and the ability to chuck a jellyfish the length of a tennis court.

Now, at my last event of the year, I was finding out

that good racing sailors were a lot better than I'd thought too. Just as I was making progress, the camera zoomed out, allowing me to see that the universe was much bigger than I'd supposed. I wasn't back where I started; I was much further back than that. There was a certain symmetry to it all.

This demonstration of my true place in the scheme of things tossed up a couple of mysteries, of course. The first was, why had someone in Porto Cervo given me Steve's number? One possibility was to annoy Steve. After further reflection, I thought maybe it was to annoy me – put me to the hassle and expense of getting here to do nothing much at all except watch other people go sailing.

Less of a conundrum was what had been going on with *Helisara*. They weren't as good as I'd spent the last fourteen-and-something years thinking they were. It wasn't a window to the pro world at all. I'd just imagined it was. If I'd followed it up – if the boat hadn't vanished from the scene, if I hadn't started to wonder how much I wanted it – I could have come to St Tropez to be disappointed years ago. And I probably wouldn't have got a date with an ex-model to help make up for it.

I'm being hard on myself again. It didn't look like I was going to manage it in St Tropez, but perhaps I really could have been a pro last time round. It would have been more difficult than I thought, and it would have been at least as lacking in glamour as I'd begun to realise while I was packing sails on *Helisara*, but I might have made it. Even so, I wouldn't have been a good pro. I could have had the blue sky, the blue sea, the T-shirt. And hovering above me every minute of every day would have been a thinks bubble with 'Don't fuck up, don't fuck up, don't fuck up . . . damn!' written in it. All I'd have been signing up to would have been years of being shouted at impatiently by people more talented than me. I'd have hated it. So my time with Dobbs would have been an ideal apprenticeship.

In the Gulf of St Tropez, the boats flew in towards a leeward mark, and the crews prepared to drop the spinnakers. On our boat, a bowman shuffled out astride the bowsprit, like a nervous kid crossing a river on a log. The boat was racing fast, and he was high above the water with not much to hold onto and a boat ready to sail straight over him if he slipped, harness notwithstanding. He released the spinnaker tack shackle, and the corner of the sail flew away, up and out, releasing the wind and leaving the sail flapping. It was gathered by the rest of the crew, and stuffed down a hatch. It had been neatly done. Presumably some mushrooms were already hard at work. Frank turned the tender upwind to follow to the next mark. As we punched into the wind and waves, we got soaked with spray. Getting soaked with warm Mediterranean spray is actually quite pleasant. It feels manly without being uncomfortable.

All this introspection. Here's a good question: if I was no good at it, if I hated my crewmate so much, if I spent so much of the time cold and unhappy, why did I pursue sailing with such zeal? Why didn't I just quit?

I don't like thinking about this – there is no answer that really reflects well on me. I was too stupid to quit. I was too unimaginative to realise that I might be better at something else. I was too slow on the uptake to really notice how badly it was going. Or maybe I just liked it. I'm not sure how much point there is in analysing it; it was an obsession, and obsessions are all about a lack of perspective – how else could I have travelled to Tarbert with such impossible expectations, or sailed to La Rochelle thinking I was Robin Knox-Johnston.

I'm still obsessive by nature. It's not enough to enjoy something; almost immediately I'll desperately want to be good at it. I was like that then; I'm like that now. To that extent I haven't changed; I've just got a little more self-knowledge. That's why I've avoided golf for years, for all the same reasons that reformed alcoholics avoid drink. I know that I'd be no good at it, and I know where it would end – with a house full of golf clubs, a soul full of angst, and an unreachable dream of getting round a golf course in fewer than one hundred strokes. In bike riding I was lucky to find something to obsess over that I could do. All of a sudden I had a work ethic. Some of these days I'm going to give up cycling, and it will be a borderline mental disorder again.[38]

That night Steve had exciting news. He'd found me a place. It was on yet another of the Wallys. Report on board in the morning. Steve looked immensely relieved at having got me off his to-do list.

The following day was simply beautiful. There was a hint of autumn in the air, but still with the warm feel of a Mediterranean morning. Shopkeepers were scrubbing pavements, the whole place was buzzing with scooters. I had breakfast outside a café by the harbour, watching as the crews worked round their boats, washing all that

[38] Yes, yes, I know I said in the first chapter that I was going to retire. Well, I haven't yet, not quite. Don't worry, people nag me about it, and I promise I'll quit soon.

disgusting dew off the deck before the owner arrived. On the classics, the crews arrived in whites, like a Fred Perry theme party. I finished my coffee and croissant, picked up my bits of sailing kit, and went to find my skipper.

I knew that this was going to be a once-only experience – I wasn't about to give up my job and run away with a sailing circus – but I enjoyed the feeling of importance that came from easing through the crowds admiring my boat, and walking confidently up the passerelle.

'Yeah, yeah, Steve said you'd be over. Good to see you,' said the skipper. 'Jason's been struggling a bit over the last few days – normally it's a two-person job, but his partner has had to go home.' He introduced me to Jason, an amiable Aussie, just like everyone else crewing the super-yachts in St Tropez. And he gave me a T-shirt, a really nice one.

The boat felt just as big and solid as *Helisara* had. Where *Helisara* had been covered with winches, blocks, tracks and ropes running everywhere, this was more modern, sleeker. There were only a third the number of winches, and most of the ropes were hidden from view. The uncluttered deck was just an expanse of immaculate teak. The mast stood above us, almost cartoonishly tall, and the boom was above head height. All the details had been thought out. This was no beast like my last maxi. This was a sexy way to go sailing. I nodded a greeting to a couple of the other crew as they came on deck.

Jason led me to the foredeck, to the edge of the deck, and jumped over the side into the tender. 'Come on,' he said.

'But I . . .' This wasn't what I'd expected.

I climbed into the tender.

'Put ya shirt on, mate. Try to look smart.'

I did so. I almost fell over as Jason jerked the throttle and the boat started forward across a harbour that was already congested with tenders and yachts.

'We're picking up the guests just at the end of the quay,' he continued.

'Guests?'

'Yeah. I think there are four of them. Tuck your shirt in. Wineglasses are in the forward locker, the cooler is back here. We've got an Aussie chardonnay, and some Spanish red. There's some beer, though we're a bit low. And there's some canapés and stuff. We usually get a sheila to do this, but you'll get the hang of it. Just give 'em a shot of your cleavage and you'll be fine.'

And so I found my niche in the world of pro yachting. Blue skies, blue seas. The T-shirt and the shades. Crisp commands and questions – the red wine or the white, sir? Even if I say so myself, I reckon I was pretty good at it.

Epilogue

THAT WAS THE END OF MY COMEBACK YEAR. AS WINTER came on, and the season ended, I realised that the most important thing of all was that, for the most part, I'd had a whale of a time. Call it perspective, if you like, and better late than never. I have some very happy memories from places like Cork or Porto Cervo or St Tropez. And the less good stuff? Well, it was never that bad. Even the disappointment of Tarbert was worth it to see Gery Trentesaux in action close up. Or at least it is in retrospect, which is all that matters now.

Certainly I'd had more actual fun than I'd ever had as a teenager. And best of all, going to St Tropez and seeing how real men sail meant that any serious ambitions I'd had were instantly rendered laughable. I could get better, I could even get worse; it really didn't matter. Sailing was just what I made of it. At last, I was doing one of the most enjoyable sports in the world for the sheer pleasure of it, because there was no other reason for me to do it.

I kept sailing. In 2007 I began the season as crew boss

on *Afterglow*, with a group of people who had become my good friends. We started to plan a Fastnet Race campaign. Sadly that fell through when Dougal received an offer to buy the boat, and decided that his responsibilities lay more towards his family's financial stability than to his friends having a good time. I continued to crew for him on a 24-footer he bought as a more economical replacement, and to pick up whatever bits of sailing I could fit in elsewhere on other boats. I don't have as much time for it as I would like.

Just occasionally I tell people about my stint as a pro in St Tropez. I've still got the T-shirt, which always impresses them.

As long as I keep my back to a wall, no one can see it says 'Hostess' on the back.

Acknowledgements

As a courtesy to those involved, I have changed most of the names of both sailors and boats. Unfortunately, this has the knock-on effect of making the help they generously gave me rather more difficult to acknowledge here than I would like.

Notwithstanding, I want to express my gratitude to the owners and skippers I sailed with: Dougal, Mac, Mike, Neil, and Gordon, all of them excellent seamen, and nice guys.

My thanks to the crews of *Afterglow*, *Blaze of Glory*, *White Osprey*, and *Moorish Idol*. You made for a great year, one that I wouldn't have missed for anything.

I also received considerable assistance from Michael Kearney, Malcolm McKeag, and Stuart Quarrie. And I'm grateful to Henri-Lloyd, manufacturers of top-grade sailing gear, who gave me generous discounts on kit.

Further back into the past, Stephen Dobbs may have been sarcastic about it, but he did at least tolerate sitting in a dinghy with me for a couple of seasons when anyone with a less masochistic instinct would have resigned. I ought also to say that we became much better friends after we stopped racing together.

My agent, Peter Buckman, was patient enough to provide encouragement through a writing process that lasted rather longer than anyone expected. At Yellow Jersey, Tristan Jones and Juliet Brooke were a joy to work with.

To my partner, Louisa, my thanks for her exceptional tolerance. And finally, thank-you to my parents, who were responsible for the whole sailing thing to begin with.